Guilt Be Gone!

Become a Proud Working Mom in 12 Easy Steps

JENNIFER BARBIN

Written by Jennifer Barbin

Edited by Annie Cosby

Cover and interior design by Annie Cosby

ISBN:1493637819

ISBN 13:9781493637812

For my girls,
Megan and Emily

Should you follow in my footsteps and someday tackle
working motherhood,
may you always find joy, balance, and meaningful work.

And for my son,
Parker

Respect, reinforce, and empower your partner to be all she
can be.
Make me proud.

• Table of Contents •

The Purpose of This Book

I have had jobs that I loved and jobs that I could have gone without. I have worked for Fortune 500 companies, large privately held companies, and even the family-owned variety. And my roles have run the gamut—marketing, direct sales, consulting, sales leadership, and hybrids of all three. But I have always worked.

As a mother of three and a traveling executive, I am often stopped by working mothers of all types: full-time, part-time, traveling, remote, in-office, and any combination of those you can imagine. And I'm always asked the same question:

How are you making it work?

It's a complicated question, and I hope that this book will provide some real answers to the issues these mothers face, particularly the one question that I think lies at the bottom of each working mother's consciousness:

How do I rid myself of the guilt that stems from working instead of staying at home with my children?

This book is for working mothers. The words on the pages that follow do not address whether it is better to work or better to stay home. We will not cover whether you work because you want to or because you have to out of financial necessity. The working- versus stay-at-home-mother question is a never-ending issue that presents unique challenges and opportunities to each family. For this reason, I choose not to tackle the question of *whether* a mother should work—but instead how she can cope with all facets of her life when she finds herself holding a job *and* raising children.

You have reached for this book because you are a working mother, dealing with the feelings of guilt that plague so many of us who struggle with the deep desire to be in two places at the same time. Through this book, I hope to help you make the most of—and feel good about—the time you have in each area of your life.

If you are a stay-at-home mom, please know that I have the utmost respect for you, and I honor what you do for your children every single day. But because my personal journey has been as a working mother, the tips and suggestions in this book reflect that experience.

To all the working mothers of the world: I hope these words find you well and bring you comfort and inspiration.

Jennifer Barbin

Any Given Monday

The alarm goes off at 5:30 a.m. I have to fight the urge to hit the snooze button.

As I drag myself out of bed and onto the treadmill, my thoughts shift to the day ahead, to the last-minute changes to the presentation I'm giving this afternoon in Chicago. Though mere hours away, the presentation feels so distant from my home office in Colorado. I wipe my face of any lingering sweat and diligently make the final edits. When it's done, I feel proud. And, more importantly, I'm ready for the conference call with my boss to give it one last review before my flight.

The coffee maker is my next priority. I flip the switch on my way back upstairs to get cleaned up for the day. As the first pot of coffee brews, I get dressed and pack some last-minute items into my suitcase.

My husband Scott has already left the house, taking most days I travel as an opportunity to get a jumpstart on his workday. This means I need to get my thirteen- and nine-year-old daughters ready for school and my four-year-old son ready for daycare before I get myself to the airport. It's a challenge, but not impossible.

When I finally have a hot cup of coffee in hand, my bags packed, and my presentation ready to go, I'm confident and excited. The kids aren't even out of bed yet, but I feel like everything is under control. For one rare moment, I feel confident that I am successfully juggling the demands of a career and motherhood. But the challenge is only just beginning.

Breakfasts are eaten, lunches made. Megan and Emily pull on sweaters and tennis shoes, and I step outside to say goodbye as they go to meet the school bus. Then I help Parker get dressed, gather his things, and we're *finally* out the door.

As Parker and I make the short drive to his daycare, I gaze into the back seat at his sweet little face. Full of innocence and energy, he still has that chubby toddler look. But it's starting to thin out. He's starting to get bigger. *Soon he'll be a little boy*, I remind myself, *and not a baby at all*.

As always, he is in a good mood, smiling and pretending, obviously involved in some sort of superhero battle as Batman, his favorite character. Today is an extra special day at daycare; they will be playing baseball, something Parker looks forward to every week. I remembered to bring his teddy bear for naptime, and we even packed up his favorite toy cars for show-and-tell. As we pull into the daycare parking lot, I silently applaud myself for how smoothly the morning has gone.

Knowing that I need to be at the airport in an hour, I pick up the pace. But the change is instantaneous. As we walk through the front doors, Parker's mood begins to plummet. He grabs onto my nicely ironed pant leg and his little face contorts with emotion, becoming clingy and sad. I pretend not to notice and keep the chipper mood going for both of our sakes. *As soon as I get him settled in, he'll be fine*, I tell myself.

I sit him down, pull out his cars and politely suggest to his teacher that she read his favorite story to divert his attention away from my ensuing departure. But Parker isn't falling for it. His round, wet eyes have now given way to giant tears.

One hour. I have one hour to get to the airport. And Parker continues to wail. It makes me feel awful. I won't see him for three days, but I *need* to leave or I'll miss my flight. I start my heartfelt goodbye and begin prying him off my leg in order to hand him over to the daycare teacher.

But before I can even think of finishing this painful departure my cell phone rings. It's my daughters' school.

Against the backdrop of Parker's loud sobs, I hear that Emily, my second grader, has a fever and needs to be picked up. I quickly phone Scott, but he is in meetings and not answering. I try our teenaged babysitter who helps us out a few days a week after school, but she has class.

I'm out of options.

My phone starts ringing again—a lifeline? Scott? Not so lucky. It's my boss.

She's expecting to review an employee situation as well as run through my looming presentation during my 45-minute drive to the airport. The drive that I haven't started yet.

My thoughts run wild. I *need* to get Parker to stop crying. I *need* to figure out what to do with Emily. I *need* to make my flight. I need my boss to at least *think* I am in control. I feel overwhelmed. I feel alone.

It's a scene familiar to any working mother. And there's only one thing to do:

Take a deep breath.

You are a professional, I tell myself. *You are paid to solve problems. Take action.*

I call Julia, a good friend of mine who is a stay-at-home mother. "I don't have time to explain, but I really need your help. Are you able to watch Emily for a few hours?"

"Of course I can take her," Julia says calmly. "We're just hanging around today. I'll make sure she gets lots of rest." We both know that I owe her a lot, and even though I want to reciprocate, the opportunity never seems to present itself. As a working mother, it is always a matter of finding the *time.*

And at this moment, even though I am so grateful to Julia, I'm also overwhelmed with pangs of jealousy and self-doubt. I'm confident that Emily is in good hands today, but I can't shake my own feelings of uncertainty.

I *should be there for my daughter when she's sick. Not someone else.*

As I contemplate this thought, I am brought back to Parker, who is still turning away from his teacher and tugging on my pant leg.

He looks at me with his big brown eyes. Between sobs he says, *"Mommy, why do you always have to go to work?"*

My Journey to Working Motherhood

I was 15 when I got my first job. Back then, I didn't know where or how far my career would go. But I knew, even then, that I would *always* work.

I'm grateful that I can say my time spent working has been the evolvement of a purpose—not just a job. But people often wonder *why* I find such pride in my work. How did I get to the point where I *want* to work? Why do I put so much stock in my career? Some suggest that the reason is because I, myself, grew up in a working mother home. And while it is true that the story of my mother's work life certainly did shape my career, it was not in the way one would think.

My mother grew up in a traditional home and *wanted* to be a stay-at-home mom. She did not have career aspirations. She did not want to accomplish anything extraordinary professionally. And she did not concern herself with finding purposeful work. Her vision was much different: she wanted to get married and spend her time nurturing her family. I very much wish she could have had this. It would have made her happy—and our family too.

My parents divorced when I was five. My mother became single almost overnight, eradicating her hope of being a stay-at-home mom. The memories I have of this time are not happy ones. I remember my mother crying a lot and pacing in our tiny two-bedroom apartment. She was constantly leaning on me, just a child, to help her figure out what to do next. She spent an enormous amount of time reflecting on the past: what hadn't worked, the mistakes she had made, and replaying over and over what she should have done differently so that we wouldn't be where we were at that moment. Nothing was ever *encouraging* or *positive*. We were always looking back and regretting—or looking forward with fear.

My mother was not a proud working mom. She was distracted, resentful and, unfortunately, never fully present. One household suddenly broken into two meant we struggled financially. We resorted to unconventional ways to make ends meet. We took in boarders to live in our basement. We searched under vending machines for spare change. We cut coupons, and wore hand-me-down clothing. It was out of control and uncertain. For a child, living this way was scary.

My mother *did* work, but she didn't enjoy it. The problem was that she never wanted to work and thusly never tried to find anything that fueled her interests. She tried to do her part to support us, but always resorted to quick fixes—jobs that did not utilize her skills, inspire her passions, or compensate in a way that provided self-respect or confidence. As a result, her various jobs never lasted long. It seemed almost deliberate—as if to reinforce the belief system she grew up with: *real mothers did not work.*

She was a waitress. She was in telesales. She worked in customer service. She had a degree in art, but none of these roles offered an opportunity to be creative. She was a working mom constantly plagued with stress and the necessity to make ends meet. Not an uncommon theme. Her working life fell into a pattern: spending months looking for a job, working for a few weeks, disliking the job, getting written up, getting fired. And so it went ...

I was ten when her depression really cemented itself, much too young to be of any real help. At the time, my younger sister and I thought she was just an unhappy single, working mother. We would later learn that her sadness was far more extreme than the daily blues. Eventually, she would be formally diagnosed with severe depression—something that was largely misunderstood at that time and thusly not properly managed or supported.

But I did what I could. I started walking dogs after school, I performed odd jobs for neighbors, and I became the go-to babysitter in the neighborhood. Then, at the age of 15, I got my first *real* job—working in a grocery store. I stocked shelves, worked the checkout, and even put in some time in the deli. And I *loved* it.

Though my earnings were small, I began to contribute money to my family. I was able to buy a few things just for me, and, for the first time, I felt *in control*. I felt powerful. Working gave me confidence, and that confidence made me feel *safe*. I knew then that I would always work.

I wish my childhood story ended well, but it doesn't. My mother lost her battle with ongoing depression, and at the age of 47, she committed suicide. Even today, more than 23 years later, it is difficult for me to write these words, much less to say them out loud.

I tell you this story to illustrate how my path to working motherhood began. People say that your history sets the path for your future. Mine certainly did for me.

Working became a way to keep myself busy and move my focus away from the things that haunted my daily life. Working kept me *safe*.

Although my childhood certainly had its moments of sorrow, it also provided something wonderful: a strong work ethic and a confidence in my abilities. I learned that if I worked at something hard enough, I could accomplish whatever goals I set. I could take care of myself, and that was empowering.

It was natural, then, that I would work my way through college at the University of Iowa. I waitressed, worked in a daycare (cementing my love for children), and worked in a library returning books to the shelves. I tried lots of jobs—

anything to pay tuition, help out with the care of my sister, and provide support to my father who, in the absence of my mother, had now assumed the role of sole parent.

In my third year of college, I met Scott. He lived down the hall, and we became good friends. Scott was a great guy—stable, smart, and conservative—everything I was not used to. We made the perfect couple.

We had a lovely wedding when I was 23, and started a happy life. We both worked and found jobs we enjoyed. We bought a little townhouse, kept sound finances, and enjoyed a fairly uncomplicated life.

I excelled at what I was doing. I worked longer and harder than anyone I knew—man or woman. At age 27, I was promoted to regional sales manager of my office, making me the youngest member of management for this Fortune 500 company and in charge of one of the largest regions. I stayed with the same company and continued my career development in a wide variety of roles, always working long hours and focusing on accomplishing more than I had before. At the age of 30, I was promoted again, this time to general manager, a position held by only a handful of other females in the company that boasted sales of over $13 billion annually. To hold this position in a sea of middle-aged men struck me as quite an achievement. I had accomplished quite a bit through hard work and dedication, and I was proud.

And then, at the age of 31, I became pregnant. We were *thrilled!* We picked a room in our house to be the baby's room. We painted it a pale pink and bought a crib. I read baby books, I Googled countless what-if scenarios, and we argued happily over names. We were ready.

Life would continue as always while at the same time becoming infinitely more exciting: I would return to work *and* I would now be a mother.

How hard could it be?

Megan was born in August of that year. She was the most beautiful child I had ever seen. She was chubby, no hair to speak of, and smelled wonderful (you know that amazing little infant smell). I felt an immediate bond with her that I had never imagined was possible. I was surprised, even shocked, by it. I loved it.

Maternity leave was glorious. This was the first time I had ever taken any real time off from work. I spent hours playing with Megan and holding her as she napped. I organized my pantry and closets, and even made meals every night for our tiny family—and I am *not* a natural cook! It was great for all three of us, and I loved the time. But I loved it as one loves a vacation; it wasn't *me*. Even after six weeks, just halfway through maternity leave, I started thinking about work. I started craving business conversations and yearned to get back in the game.

That's when I had my first taste of *working mother guilt*.

The passive-aggressive statements from friends and strangers alike began to surface.

"*I hope you're not exhausted all the time.*" But I had been exhausted before I was ever pregnant. I reasoned that I could get along fine without a great deal of sleep. "*I hope you can manage the feedings, the sleepless nights, and all the diaper changes—it will be rough.*" But they had no idea that I was quite experienced at multi-tasking, I wasn't worried. "*But do you think you will be able to give your job the real focus it requires?*" It was interesting to note that Scott never received any of these questions. I guess everyone assumed I would take on the majority of new parent responsibilities.

"*And there's no way you could possibly stay home?*" people would ask. It felt that everywhere I turned, people were expressing skepticism or sympathy around the idea of me returning to work. *Wanting* to return to my job was not even something to be contemplated. The world seemed to be telling me that *wishing* to work and wanting to continue to develop a career as a working mother was wrong.

Everywhere I went, I was approached by women, by men, by strangers. They asked me, "Who is going to watch your kids when you're working?"

"We found a great daycare," I would answer confidently, hoping the conversation was over.

JENNIFER BARBIN

They continued, "But how can you leave that little one in the care of someone else?" The questions hurt. They hurt a lot—I loved my child. But I liked working, too. Was this really so strange?

So I did what any self-respecting new mother would do. I lied. Or, as I like to think of it, I began telling small fibs. I explained—again and again—that I *had* to go back, that our finances required it. I knew this wasn't the truth. We weren't wealthy and would have had to make adjustments, but I could have stayed home if I wanted to. *I knew that I was* choosing *to work.*

In those early weeks of Megan's life, I reflected quite a bit on my own mother. I kept thinking of how she would have loved the opportunity to simply stay home and look after Megan. Instead, I was choosing to reject her dream lifestyle and put a stiff suit on every day. I wondered if she would have been envious of my choices, or disappointed in my decisions.

It took much internal debate, but my decision to go back to work after having Megan came down to two crucial facts, in this order:

1) I had worked very hard to get my career to where it was.

2) *Working made me happy.*

After ten weeks, I ended my maternity leave and went back—two weeks early. At the time, I was the only female employee at the company who had ever gone back to work *before* maternity leave was up.

Despite the fact that it was my decision, it was still conflicting. Each night I would sneak into Megan's room. I would peek into her crib and gaze at her tiny face and realize that she had experienced a full day that I wasn't a part of. And my mind would reel.

Maybe I am a bad mother because I work.

Maybe my mother was right to want to stay home.

Maybe I'm being selfish.

The cycle of working mother guilt had only just begun.

What is Working Mother Guilt?

"Show me a woman who doesn't feel guilty and I'll show you a man."

Erica Jong

•Proud Working Moms Confess•

"I was so stressed out that I either had to give up my career or not be able to be the mother I wanted to be. The guilt literally made me feel sick."

Emily

Marketing assistant and mother of one

"I worry that my children's teachers know them better than me. I worry that they feel lonely and neglected when I'm not there. I worry that I can't make homemade meals every night. I worry that Caden is still too little to tell me how he feels about me working, but if he could, would he tell me that he misses me? Would he wish I would stay home with him? I wonder if I'm being selfish by working because I want to, and not because I have to. I worry that my choice to work will have a detrimental impact on my kids. Will they turn out okay even though they went to daycare instead of being home with their mother? Am I a good mother?"

Juliette

Sales executive and mother of two

•What is Working Mother Guilt?•

I have been there.
I am there, right now.
Every. Single. Day.

If you have ever felt torn between motherhood and your job, you are not alone. Almost every working mother struggles with feelings of persistent and sometimes overwhelming guilt. It weighs heavily on our conscience, making us question our very sense of self. It makes us doubt both our parenting and our career choices. Working mother guilt is real.

Working mothers often exhaust themselves trying to manage their personal lives while also being successful in their careers. Unable to balance it all perfectly, the guilt sets in, filling us with self-doubt when what we really need is the extra motivation to help us carry on.

We come in all shapes and forms; some of us work full-time, some work part-time, some work out of an office, some travel, and some work from home. Many *choose* to work, wanting to develop a career and pursue passions outside of family, and still others see working only as a means to an end. Regardless of which category you might find yourself in, we all struggle with the same thing: how to cope with the feelings of guilt that stem from the need to be in two places at once and the reality that it is just not possible.

Guilt is unproductive. It's unforgiving and a huge waste of time. We all intuitively know this, but the relentless, nagging question is always there:

"Is it all worth it?"

Sometimes, the feelings are as big and bright as billboards directly in front of us. But other times they're just passive undertones we feel when we defend our choices to questioning co-workers, family members, or even good friends. All of this questioning and defending stems from misdirected feelings of wrong-doing or fault.

This is working mother guilt.

I get it. Today, with three children of my own, I understand all too well the challenges of being a working mother. I rush home from work to get the kids to practice or to a game. I also need to help with homework, clear the house of its never-ending mess, perform nightly counseling sessions to smooth over the latest social disaster, and somewhere in between all of that, I find time for a family dinner.

At work, I have an entirely different set of struggles. As executive vice president of sales for a large company, I am responsible for traveling across the country, strategizing, developing and delivering large presentations, and most importantly, managing a wide range of personalities. The changing issues, alternating temperaments, and requirements can sometimes seem endless.

And then there is the intangible stuff: the judgment. No matter how often you tell people, "I am a better mother because I work," there will always be people who don't agree, and don't agree *loudly*. And even if you *do* find support from other people, this guilt can come not only from others—but also from within.

After many years of fighting contradictory feelings of regret and pride, I now feel that I have found the perfect balance. Am I still occasionally resentful that some of the daily tasks I undertake seem more easily accomplished by stay-at-home moms? Yes. Do I feel envious or guilty that this is not the life I live? Not anymore. *Why?*

I live an amazing "double life." I have a fulfilling role in my career *and* a deeply rewarding family environment.

As you will learn, finding happiness in the chaos and struggle of working motherhood requires a layered approach. From motivation to resources, this book will give you the strategies to balance the demands of your contrasting roles as a working woman and as a mother, while helping alleviate the guilt so many women feel from trying to accomplish too much.

This book is for any working mother who continues to feel guilt from any direction in her life. In these pages, you will find answers. You will not learn how to be a perfect mother. In fact, there is no such thing. But you *will* learn how to strive towards excellence as you define it, not impossible perfection. By shifting your attitude, making simple adjustments, and learning not to take yourself so seriously, you too will leave your guilt behind and become a happy and proud working mom.

So let's get started!

One

Embrace
Childcare

"You are worried about seeing him spend his early years in doing nothing. What! Is it nothing to be happy? Nothing to skip, play, and run around all day long? Never in his life will he be so busy again."

Jean Jacques Rousseau

•Proud Working Moms Confess•

"I was so nervous.
I couldn't believe I was leaving the love of my life and my most prized person in the hands of a stranger."

Helen
Advertising representative and mother of two

"My son didn't start daycare until he was two years old. However, I was terrified to leave him while I went to work. I hadn't ever heard good things about daycare. My mother was a single mom with three kids and never would have let us attend daycare. But for me it has been an amazing experience. My son has learned so much there. He gets to socialize and interact with kids his own age. Daycare is one of the best decisions I've made, and I think that even if I wasn't working I would want my son to go a few days a week for the experience and interaction."

Julie
Real estate agent and mother of two

One

· Embrace Childcare ·

Childcare has always been a huge source of guilt for me. So much so that once, much to my embarrassment, I found myself *pretending* to be a stay-at-home mom.

It was one morning when Emily, my middle child, was not feeling well. I left work early to take her to the doctor, but on my way to pick her up, I did something crazy: I changed into jeans and tennis shoes.

I was only planning on being at the doctor's office for a few hours. Then, as long as she was doing better, I was going to return her to our nanny. So why would I take the time to change out of my business suit and put on a set of casual clothes?

Openly, I would tell people that I did it for comfort. Pantyhose, heels, and a suit will wear on any woman, especially while trying to lug around a baby carrier. But in truth, I did it because I wanted everyone to think well of me, that I was a "good and fully dedicated mom."

As I was making the quick change in the car, I called Scott on my cell. I told him what I was doing. Understandably, he thought I was going overboard. Of course he did, because—and I mean this in a loving way— my husband is a man.

If *he* rushes into a doctor's appointment in a suit, he is considered a wonderful and dedicated father—a man supporting his family and willing to take time out of his busy work schedule for his sick daughter. But if *I* rushed in and gave the impression that I was planning to return to a work environment immediately following Emily's doctor appointment, well, I suspected my dedication to my daughter would be called into question.

I could almost hear the statements coming from the pediatrician and supporting staff:

"You're going to go back to work while she isn't feeling well?"

"Maybe Emily wouldn't have gotten sick if she hadn't spent so much time in daycare."

"Are you sure you have a handle on all of her symptoms? You know, since she isn't with you all day?"

"We understand that you need to get back to work, but the antibiotics we are giving take at least 24 hours to work; you aren't just planning on bringing her back to daycare are you?"

So what did I do to avoid the above? I lied. Maybe I didn't really *lie*, but I certainly pretended.

The reality was that my doctor was *not* thinking that I was a horrible mom. He wasn't judging me—I was just wildly insecure. None of this was necessary, because I wasn't doing anything wrong. I had resorted to putting on a pair of jeans to fix my own confidence issues. I have come a *long* way since then. You will too.

Childcare should not be a source of guilt. In fact, it's one of a working mother's best resources. But you have to learn to embrace it as such. Unfortunately, contrasting opinions can sometimes make this difficult.

I started researching childcare almost the moment I learned I was pregnant the first time. My strategy: carefully consider each of the options at hand. In business, this had always worked well for me. So I looked into them all: daycare centers, nannies, in-home care, out-of-home care. I spoke to mothers, grandmothers, teachers, and even a few dads. In this case, however, I learned the hard way what a sensitive subject childcare really is.

Maybe I spoke with the wrong people or maybe I unconsciously sought out contrary opinions to my own beliefs, but I certainly received more negative than positive feedback. So much so that it started to weigh on my mind—constantly. I questioned my objectives and who I was. I let everyone else's opinions influence what they thought I should do.

But I pressed on, made my decision, and after 12 weeks, it was time for Megan to start daycare. The trouble was that for months I had been listening to everyone listing the terrible effects daycare had on children. So I entered into what should have been an exciting new phase of our life with a negative mindset. I began childcare thinking I was bringing harm to Megan, never considering all the good it could provide.

And it was terrible. Every morning, I dropped Megan off and sheepishly snuck out of the center to begin my morning commute. I had built up this negative idea of daycare to such heights that simply driving to work made me feel like a horrible mother. I was abandoning my child!

My outlook on childcare flowed into my workday, which resulted in my feeling embarrassed and avoiding daycare discussions with co-workers. I assumed they were judging me, sure that I was focusing on my career at the expense of my baby.

But even worse than my own insecurities were all the daycare horror stories told to me by my fellow (well-meaning) co-workers. *Did you hear that story of the child who was left outside for hours? Did you hear about the teacher who set the baby on fire?* I knew Megan was colicky and could be difficult, this only exacerbated my concerns. I imagined she spent the entire day crying, fussing in her crib, and refusing her teachers' attention. I imagined the teachers were becoming frustrated with her and responding with indifference, or even worse, negative discipline.

Are they taking good care of her? What if they treat her poorly? How can I really know? What if they play favorites and Megan isn't one of them? Are they *raising her instead of* me? Or the mother lode of a working mom's fears: *What if she grows to like them better than me?*

All in all, I worried that I was failing. *I worried I was a bad mother.*

After many years and lots of time spent on this subject, I know now that I couldn't have been farther from the truth. In reality, there was nothing wrong with leaving Megan in daycare. She was thriving, learning, and having fun. I was not a bad mother. I was, and am, a working mother. In fact, I was being the very best mother I could possibly be.

Being the best mother meant mothering in the way that worked for *me*. I had to be me. But it would take me some time—and numerous strategies—to figure this out. The rest of this chapter is devoted to sharing these strategies with you.

Having mixed feelings about surrendering your childcare duties to other caretakers is normal. You may worry that you're abandoning your responsibilities, or worse, abandoning your child—but you are not. In fact, using childcare can help you be a great mother. And it's an incredible advantage that was not available to mothers in past generations.

Seek solace in the fact that you are not alone. Childcare is becoming a common element for many families. According to the National Center for Educational Statistics, an estimated 13 million children younger than six spend some, or all, of their day being cared for by someone other than their parents. This includes babies and toddlers.

Whether you *want* to go back to work or *need* to work so you can support your family, remember this:

Working does not make you any less of a mother. Not even close.

In fact, the lesson I learned from childcare—*that it is far from an awful thing*—runs contrary to the many opinions that I should not have wasted time listening to. Being a devoted and loving mom does not require you to be with your baby all day. *Being a devoted and loving mom only requires that you always provide love.*

Below are two important tactics I used to become comfortable with my children being in childcare:

Realize your child is not miserable without you

I know the scenario playing in your head:

You drop off your precious darling at daycare, say goodbye, and head off to work. But then doubt sets in. You imagine that your child is crying, missing you, misbehaving, and breaking down in front of his teachers, or worse—in front of other parents.

But you have to remember: young children are both easily distracted and incredibly resilient. Maybe your child is upset for a few minutes, but oftentimes, starting a new project, reading a favorite story, or playing with a new toy is enough to divert his or her attention and make your child happy again. And good daycare teachers know this. Once you have put in the hard work and found the right place (which we'll discuss in the next chapter), know your child is all right and let it go.

If you still can't shake the idea that your child is miserable while you are at work, try other strategies to help yourself feel more comfortable. Consider asking your child's caregiver to either place a phone call to update you mid-morning, or even take pictures during the day and send them to you by email. The teachers at Megan's daycare would often take these extra steps for me and place an afternoon call coupled with a few photos of her playing dress-up or enjoying circle time. This went a long way toward keeping my own guilt and anxieties in check.

Study the benefits of childcare

As long as your children are loved and cared for they will thrive regardless of whether or not you work outside the home. But if you're still struggling with embracing childcare, research the benefits for children in childcare.

According to the University of Missouri Extension, there is no evidence that children of working mothers develop any differently than children with mothers who stay at home. Actually, numerous studies have shown that children can *benefit* significantly by spending time in childcare while their parents work. *What?* Yes, it's true!

The benefits cited include socialization skills, more mature immune systems, and even academic advantages. I have provided more commonly cited benefits to get you started:

Independence

Children who have positive experiences separating from their parents earlier in life learn to trust that their parents will leave, but that they will always come back.

Every time I drop Parker at daycare, I say, "I love you, and I will see you soon!"

These short separations actually help build confidence in his own abilities and ultimately help him become a more self-reliant and thriving individual.

Socialization

There is no better social interaction for small children than being with other small children and having the opportunity to learn, play, and be accepting and tolerant of each other.

Siblings are great companions, but there are social benefits to your children playing in groups with others their age. That's where daycare comes in handy. Where else can a group of three-year-olds play together with organized activities?

I take great joy in picking Parker up and seeing him engaged in Batman or fireman dress-up games. He is with his friends and deeply involved in play, all under supervision in a safe and creative environment. Megan developed great friendships during her time at daycare. At only two years old, she made friends with two other little girls who, to this day, are still her very best friends.

Academic advantages

In a quality childcare environment, children also gain important intellectual and communication skills.

The National Institute of Child Health & Human Development funded a study to examine the effect of childcare experiences on children's cognitive, language, social, and emotional development. The study found that higher-quality care actually *contributed* to improved cognitive and language skills.

I am certain this is true. Before Parker started daycare, I would respond to his slightest grunt to meet his every need. But at daycare, we all learned that Parker had to "use his words"—his teachers pushed him to vocalize his requests. He was speaking before we knew it!

Preparation for school years

I never considered that going to daycare would make my children's transitions into the school years easier for *me*! For many mothers, the school transition is incredibly difficult. If their children have been home with them every day for five years, starting school can be very difficult for both the mother and the child. In this sense, I consider myself very lucky.

Megan, Emily, and Parker spent their toddler years in organized childcare. Because of this, their transition to full-day kindergarten was easier on all of us. All three of my kids have great social skills and have learned to be comfortable both in group settings and on their own. Parker has always loved coming home and sharing his day with me, telling me all about his new friends and activities. The experience has been happy for both of us, not met with resistance or stress.

Structure and routine

I know enough about myself to know that if I stayed home with my children, I would not regularly structure play dates, learning time, or age-appropriate art projects. It's just not one of my strong points! But, in daycare, all of these things are consistently provided for children.

When your kids are home with you all day, it can be easy to run out of fun activities, projects, and places to visit. Let's admit it—television can become a steady source of entertainment if we are not careful. But, in childcare, there is always something to do and someone to play with.

I am routinely astonished by the impressive structure and routine of Parker's daycare. One example is when I drop by and see a group of four-year-olds actively putting all of their toys away. The teacher explained that this is simply part of the routine. The children know that first they put the toys away, and then they have snack time. What a wonderful example of structure! We have taken to trying this at home now, too.

Respect for authority

In our home, Mom and Dad are in charge. However, at daycare, all of my children have learned to obey and respect *other* adults. This is an important life lesson they were fortunate to learn at an early age.

I have a friend who is always surprised when the daycare workers comment on how focused and well-behaved her daughter is in daycare. She has been tempted at times to ask if they are sure they have the right child! The truth is that children will frequently behave better when they are with other authority figures than when they are at home. *Why?*

One reason is peer pressure. Your child wants to be perceived by teachers and by others as "good." The second reason is that there is a security in most children that the love from a parent is unconditional. And though this security is a very positive thing, the result is that the child may be more likely to misbehave in the home environment than in the childcare facility.

No matter what you choose, remember that you are still your child's essential caregiver—the most consistent source of love and support in his or her life.

Childcare is not a bad thing. In business as well as your personal life, if you just stop for a minute and consider your situation objectively, you already know the answer:

You are a smart, empowered, and busy working mother. Follow your instincts, as you always have, and bask in your success!

Two

Choose
the
Right Type
of
Childcare

"A willing partner for working moms, she comforts, pampers, soothes and calms. With all the love she has to share, she's great to have when Mommy can't be there."

Unknown

•Proud Working Moms Confess•

"I approached my daycare search just like a job hunt. I was thorough; I did my homework and I started early."

Kalli

Real estate agent and mother of three

"In my opinion, the most important thing when evaluating childcare is the tenure of the teachers or caregivers at the location. You are not looking for the number of years of total experience, rather, how long they have been at the particular center or location."

Heidi

Marketing assistant and mother of one

"My daycare provider is very good. She has an in-home daycare, it is very organized, clean, and she loves the kids. I can tell they love her too. If given the choice, I would do it again and again."

Nancy

Dental assistant and mother of one

Two

• Choose the Right Type of Childcare •

Finding high-quality childcare that both you and your little one are comfortable with will erase your feelings of uncertainty and help eradicate mommy guilt. But the type of childcare you choose depends on any number of variables: cost, hours, child-teacher ratio, and distance from home or work. So it's important to spend time finding the right childcare for your situation.

Because there are so many options, fully inspecting your childcare alternatives can seem like both an overwhelming and a daunting task, especially if you're already maintaining a full-time work schedule. However, taking the time to really think about these options from the perspective of what you and your family need will be one of the most important steps a guilt-free working mother can make.

This chapter lists the seven tactics I used to find childcare for my children. I hope it will help you choose the best form for *your* family, whatever that looks like.

Ask questions and get answers

As a professional, you would never go into a meeting unprepared. Childcare is no different! As my old manager used to say, "Get the facts and the facts will set you free!"

When it came to making my childcare choices, I painstakingly interviewed ten daycares, five in-home centers, and a handful of nannies. I wanted to see the similarities and differences, understand their atmospheres, and compare pricing.

The more I stopped by and saw different childcare facilities in action, the more comfortable I became with the idea of leaving my baby with a caregiver when I returned to work. Seeing different styles of childcare options also helped me to determine what type of childcare I was looking for.

As you investigate options, be sure to check all facilities in a disciplined way. Before starting your search, prepare a list of questions to ask each potential caregiver. Be sure that you are aware of your concerns, wants, and expectations—and then don't be afraid to voice them.

At the end of this chapter I have included two childcare resources for you. One is a list of different types of childcare and the advantages and disadvantages associated with each. You'll also find a list of childcare-related questions to guide you when you have narrowed your decision down to a few choices. Take these questions with you when you visit potential facilities to get some answers that will be important factors in your decision. These lists are by no means all-inclusive, but should certainly provide you with a great start.

Consider work hours and location

This should be a major part of your decision process, but surprisingly, it is often not given full consideration. Having a senior position with significant responsibility and the hours to match created a conundrum for me: how could I spend some daylight hours with my child and still put in the time needed to be successful?

My answer: I chose a daycare close to my office because it gave me a great sense of peace knowing that I was able to check in on Megan at any time, if only for a few minutes. I checked in at lunch or sometimes even in the early afternoon. She was happy and thriving, and I felt like I could dedicate my days to work without missing out on her development.

Consider your work hours and location before making your decision. Do you need a childcare provider closer to work, or does it make more sense to have your provider closer to your home?

Maybe taking your children along for the commute will foster great quality time. Alternatively, the drive time could also give you the chance to accomplish work tasks, or even have a little down time for yourself. Will you be the sole person responsible for transportation to and from daycare, or will you have a spouse or family members helping? If it's a group effort, maybe a location near home would be more convenient for your support group.

Each has its advantages and disadvantages, so start by walking through your typical daily routine.

Have a back-up plan

When it comes to young children, working moms know to expect the unexpected. One particularly challenging time for me happened when I was on a business trip in Chicago.

My cell phone rang and, sure enough, it was my daycare. Emily had a fever and needed to come home right away. Scott was unreachable, and Emily needed to be picked up within the hour due to daycare policy. While I respect and appreciate keeping only healthy children on-site, picking up your child without notice can be very difficult, especially when your job requires travel.

We were stranded. I was 1,000 miles away and felt very alone. It was only after 45 minutes of phoning every friend imaginable that I came to a solution. Looking back, had I developed a stronger back-up plan—maybe a relative or a standby babysitter on call—this situation would have gone much smoother.

Whatever childcare type you choose, whether it be a daycare, nanny, au pair, or relative, make sure you have a thoughtful back-up plan. What will you do when your child gets sick and can't go to the childcare facility or in-home daycare for the day? What will happen if your in-home provider is sick and needs to take a day off? What if your in-home provider wants to take a vacation during dates other than your planned family trip?

Be sure that you have considered and created back-up plans to handle unexpected situations.

Consider your budget

It really goes without saying that cost should not be the determining factor when finding quality care for your child. However, it is an inevitable consideration and you need to make sure you have budgeted for this expense.

You also need to consider all the "extras" very carefully. My daycare has always had late-pickup fees for each child past 6 p.m. With three little ones, being even a few minutes late can really add up! Some daycares do not cover lunch or breakfast, or may request you chip in for supplies.

Additionally, some have stringent policies limiting the number of weeks a child can be away for vacations without a financial penalty. As a matter of fact, Parker's daycare only allows one week off per year. Our family usually takes two weeks of vacation, so we pay the daycare for a whole week each year that Parker isn't even there. Although frustrating, it was easier for me to come to terms with it because I understood the policy upfront. This limited number of "free" weeks comes as a surprise to many new mothers and might make other childcare options more attractive or affordable.

It should be noted that these hidden fees are not limited to daycare centers. Many in-home providers and nannies expect vacation pay, reimbursement for daily lunches, mileage, or other expenses. Don't stress over these details, just make sure you know the full cost of your child's care *before you commit.*

Take a test drive

When I narrowed my choice of childcare options down to daycare, I had to choose between two different locations. To the surprise of many, I brought six-week-old Megan to each center for a half day. I watched how they interacted with her, cared for the other children, and worked with each other. *Is it a happy environment? Are the babies content and cared for? Are they loved?*

Pay attention to how staff members or your prospective nanny interacts with your child and the other children. If you don't see them at the children's level playing, reading, or participating, then move on to your other options.

Ultimately, I chose the daycare that was about half a mile farther from where I worked because I felt more comfortable with who would be Megan's primary teacher. Interestingly, the center was not rated as high and it wasn't "as pretty," but it just felt better for *me*.

Good teachers don't mind this step—in fact, they will welcome it. For me, it was a tremendous learning experience that helped me visualize life with childcare and made me feel more comfortable with it. Don't worry about what other people may think about you. Take this extra step to feel more comfortable in your choice.

Drop by and spy

After you have chosen a childcare provider, make sure you continue to check in. Make unannounced visits as often as you want or need to. With my own daycare center just minutes from my office, I often stop by when I am not traveling.

This is a good practice, but be forewarned: just as everything does not go perfectly when your child is at home, the same is true for your childcare provider. I used to pop in and see Emily happily playing on the floor with other children, full of smiles, but I also saw her in full meltdown while her teachers tried to get her down for a nap.

The key is that your center should be open and welcoming to your visits. Crazy things can happen during the day, but as long as your childcare provider can roll with it and maintain a good attitude, you will feel good about it, too.

Get to know your caregivers

We've all heard a fellow mother say it: "Aren't you worried your child will want to be with their teachers more than you?" Feelings of jealousy toward a child's caregiver is extremely common for a working mother. Common or not, such jealousy is silly.

Childcare should be viewed as an opportunity for our children to learn to feel safe and confident with someone other than just Mom or Dad. It's a good thing. Support your caregivers and encourage the development of great relationships with your children that are all their own.

The best way to do this is to get to know your caregiver—before you enroll. It will help you relax if you feel you really know him or her, and it will help you make your childcare decision. So have discussions with each caregiver on how they intend to handle tough situations, like separation sadness. But also remember that just as the teachers are developing their own relationships with your children, they also do things differently than you, and that is okay.

One of the most difficult issues I had with getting comfortable with daycare for Megan was getting over my fear that her teachers didn't know her secrets. They did not know that she liked having a pacifier handed to her upside down, or that she often preferred having one sock on and one sock off while napping. It's true, they did not know nor did they necessarily feel the same concern I felt for these little nuances. But children are surprisingly adaptive. Good caregivers will find their own way – and might even surprise you with new secrets they learn along the way.

Once you've made your childcare decision, it's important to continue to acknowledge your caregiver. Have brief chats when you pick your child up, send notes of appreciation, and absolutely acknowledge him or her on teacher appreciation day. Starbucks cards are my go-to gift of choice.

Finding the right childcare for you and your little ones does not need to be stressful. Simply approach it in a logical manner, as you would any work situation. By thinking through the important factors carefully and considering each and every option, you're sure to find the perfect fit. This, added to embracing the idea of childcare, puts you firmly on the road to abolishing working mother guilt.

Summary of Childcare Options

Daycare Centers

Advantages:

    Possibly more affordable than a full-time nanny

    Reliable (won't call in sick)

    Multiple adults watching: teachers, director, and other parents

    Kids have a structured day largely designed around developmental stages

    Children will learn from one another (potty training, speaking, reading, etc.)

    Kids get to socialize with other children of the same age group

    Staff members are trained in early childhood education

    Secure (buildings are locked and a code is needed to enter/exit)

    Licensed and regulated

Disadvantages:

    Caregivers care for more than one child

    Recommended ratios are typically 1 to 3 for babies and 1 to 4 for toddlers, but requirements vary from state to state

    Lower adult-to-child ratio than nanny or home daycare option

    Centers that care for infants can be hard to find (or full) so you must plan ahead

    Kids get sick more often in group care than alone

    Most centers won't provide care for sick children

    Closed during most holidays

    Rigid pickup and drop-off times

    Often fees for late pick ups

Home Daycare

Advantages:

    Often a nurturing and homelike atmosphere

    Smaller groups of children than at large daycare centers

    Usually less expensive than most other childcare options

    Usually more flexible pickup and drop-off times than a center

Disadvantages:

    If provider gets sick, you may be left in the lurch

    Kids get sick more often in group care than alone

    Many providers don't have formal schooling in early childhood education

    No caregiver supervision

    Often have to plan your vacation when home daycare takes vacation

    Less stringent licensing requirements

    Day not as structured; maybe too much technology time

    Closed for holidays and vacations

Nanny

Advantages:

    Children get very personalized attention

    Less hassle (no early a.m. pickups)

    If your child is a late sleeper, you don't have to wake him/her

    High adult-to-child ratio and focused attention

    Less germ exposure (this also can be viewed as a negative)

    Flexibility to set your own rules with caregiver

regarding feeding, discipline, sleep time, etc.

Children stay in familiar surroundings

Disadvantages:

Most expensive childcare option

There is nobody supervising the nanny when you are at work

Limited opportunities to socialize; playtime with other children must be specially arranged

Extensive paperwork and taxes (read about hiring a nanny legally)

It is on you to check the details: background checks, employment eligibility, etc.

Can leave you in the lurch if he or she quits, becomes sick, or is otherwise unavailable

Family/Relative

Advantages:

More personalized attention

Caregiver has personal interest in your child—loves and cares for him/her

The emotional bonds will last a lifetime

You may share the same values

Very inexpensive (the care may even be free)

Very reliable

Disadvantages:

Employee-employer relationship is hard to establish with a relative

The relative will earn the right to a strong, vocal opinion of how to raise your child—not a "no strings attached" model

May be hard to maintain appropriate boundaries

Your childcare philosophies may conflict
Playtime with other children must be specially
arranged, either by your or your relative
No caregiver supervision or regulation
If it doesn't work out, there may be hard feelings
Older relatives may have a hard time handling active
toddlers

Stay-at-Home Parenting

Advantages:

Mom and Dad are always the very best caregivers
You get to be there for your child's developmental
milestones
You control the quality of the care
You don't have to explain your rules or parenting
philosophy to others
You avoid the work/family tug-of-war

Disadvantages:

Possible isolation and loneliness, especially if you give
up a job you cherished or don't know many other stay-
at-home parents
Physical and emotional strain on you
Playtime with other children must be specially
arranged
Taking time off from a career can hurt your future
employment options and lifetime earning potential
Loss of income and benefits—you may need to make
lifestyle changes

Questions to Ask at Potential Childcare Facilities

Availability

What ages do you serve?

What are the drop-off and pickup times?

What holidays do you observe?

Do you offer full-time *and* part-time care?

Can I visit the facility without an appointment?

What is your sick policy?

What is the procedure should my child become sick?

Facility Questions

Is your facility licensed?

Do you have a list of references that I can call?

How long have you been in business?

What is the caregiver-to-child ratio?

Do you offer early childhood development?

Are teachers trained in first aid and CPR?

What is your staff turnover rate?

Are background checks completed on staff members?

Do you offer transportation? If so, from what locations?

How many children does your facility serve?

What are the age groups? How are they kept together or separated?

Are animals allowed on site?

Are immunizations required?

Do you dispense medication only with a parent or doctor's signature?

Cost

Do you accept any kind of financial aid?
Is there a reduction in fees if my child takes vacation?
Is there a sibling discount?
What is the fee for picking up my child late?

Daily Schedules

What does a daily schedule look like?
What time is naptime? Lunchtime?
What activities will be available for my child?
Do they play with age-appropriate toys?
Will my child leave the facility for field trips or playtime?
Do you have a place to play outside?
How much time do the children spend watching television during the day?

Mealtimes

What meals are provided?
Are snacks provided?
Are parents given a monthly menu?
Do you accommodate special dietary needs?
How do you keep breast milk stored and notated?

Care Philosophy

When do you expect toilet training? Do you help with this?
How do you engage with discipline?
What is your educational philosophy?
How often are the toys and bedding washed?
Do the caregivers use gloves when changing diapers or handling food?

Three

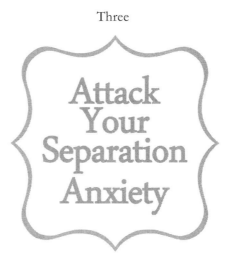

Attack Your Separation Anxiety

"A daughter may outgrow your lap, but she will never outgrow your heart."

Unknown

•Proud Working Moms Confess•

"My defining moment was when my oldest daughter was four. I traveled as part of my job since she was born, but for some reason, this trip was different. She cried and pounded her tiny fists on the floor, literally blocking the doorway with her tiny little frame. It was awful. She let me know just how mad she was that I was leaving."

Julie

Airline attendant and mother of two

"The sitter has arrived and I have my list of errands in my hand. I fly out the door and get started. Independence! I feel great. I can run to the store without the baby carrier wearing down my shoulder. No worries about where to stash that poopy diaper. I can get a latte and maybe even read a magazine. Ten minutes in and I start worrying. Will the sitter know how to make my son laugh? What if he gets hungry and she forgets how to feed him? What if he really needs me and I am not there? A thousand questions run through my mind. I end up back home within an hour."

Natalie

Mother of one

Three
• Attack Your Separation Anxiety •

Even after being a working mother for more than thirteen years, I still find long separations away from my children to be a challenge. Being away, whether for only a few hours or for days, can create tremendous guilt if not managed correctly.

I remember one Monday morning when Emily was about five years old. We had just finished a wonderful weekend, and, just like any family, we all had the Monday blues. I had a business trip planned and was finishing packing while trying to get everyone ready for the day. Emily was tired, she wasn't in the mood for school, and the idea of me heading out on another work trip just added to the negative vibe we had going.

I was in a hurry and made a series of bad decisions.

First, I could see she was a little down, and I, too, was a bit low-spirited, knowing that I was on my way out of town and away from my family for a few days. So, I made the classic mistake so many guilt-ridden working mothers do: I cut a deal with my five-year-old. I told her that if she would get dressed faster, I would take her through the McDonald's drive-thru and get her whatever she liked. *Bad mommy.*

Really, there were three mistakes made: I broke away from our usual routine, I overdramatized my departure, *and* I offered bribes. Emily sensed all of this—my haste, the break from our routine, and my guilt. So what happened?

As you could probably predict, it didn't end well. We pulled into McDonald's and Emily, sensing the change, became upset. As we paid at the drive-thru window, she yelled out that she did not want to go to school, and that she wanted me to be a "stay-at-home mommy." Although I am at peace with my decision to be a working mother, hearing this from my children still stings.

Once we arrived at school, my poor choices continued to flow. I spent way too much time getting her settled in, setting up her breakfast, and reminding her that I would "*be gone for* only *a few days.*" I even read her a story. As you might imagine, my extra efforts only made the situation worse.

Emily started pulling on my skirt, begging me not to leave her. And then, in full theatrical display, she threw her breakfast on the floor, grapes rolling everywhere, for all to see.

I stayed a while longer, trying to make her feel better and calm down, but eventually I had to leave, with Emily still in hysterics.

I should have driven to work but instead sat in my car feeling sorry for myself. After a few minutes of heavy working mother guilt, I decided I would make a drastic change. *I would resign from my job.*

It was a job that gave me great pleasure and purpose, and a job I had worked very hard to earn. But working mother guilt had gotten the best of me.

I wiped my smeared makeup, adjusted my tear-stained jacket and re-entered the school. I walked back into the classroom and to my incredible surprise, Emily was *happily* drawing with some of her friends. She looked up and immediately ran over to hug me and show me her creation. I admired her picture and said hello to her friends. And this time, when we said goodbye, Emily hugged me and headed back to her friends almost with indifference. She was happy and engaged. She wanted to be there.

Did Emily realize how sad she was making me feel that day? She absolutely did. This is when I realized *the problem resided with me.*

We all know that children have an uncanny ability to manipulate their parents better than anyone. Despite knowing this to be true, I've still spent a lot of time trying to eliminate this as a primary source of my guilt. Remember—it's not just the child who experiences separation anxiety. That anxiety is coming from you, too!

And you are not alone in this. In a *Working Mother* survey, 67% of the working moms surveyed experienced separation anxiety when they returned to work. So, although your baby will be fine (I promise this is the case), it might take a while for *you* to adjust.

Dealing with a child's separation anxiety is another story. Children cry when their parents leave them with a sitter or daycare provider for a variety of reasons. Some children have more trouble with separations than others. Some are at different stages of development. And some know that crying gets Mom and Dad to delay leaving—or even provide guilt-gifts and attention (remember my McDonald's story).

Although the reasons are different, the good news is that *rarely* is the crying an indicator of something more serious. As long as your child is in good care, your decision to work should not have any direct negative impact on your child—hence there is no reason to feel guilty.

Here are a few facts I came across on this topic that gave me comfort knowing that children having trouble with separations is very normal:

o Usually, child separation anxiety tends to begin somewhere between months 8-12 and can last through the second year of life. This fact has been consistent with all of my kids, as our difficult times usually ended once they passed the age of three. It is just a phase ... I promise!

o Pediatricians and child development experts say that separation anxiety is an important emotional milestone for children—even though it doesn't feel that way for moms. This means that if your little one cries when you leave for work, your child is *normal*.

o Separation anxiety is a healthy sign that your child has deeply attached to you and is now aware of what is familiar and what is not. So, what is really happening when Parker gets upset from my morning departure is his feeling anxious around the unfamiliar. This should be viewed as a good thing.

The big point: Dealing with separation anxiety (for moms and children) largely rests with *how* separation is managed. Learning how to address these periods will make it easier on everyone. Use the ideas below and watch your guilt fade away!

Start separations small and do trial runs

Going back to work or leaving for an extended period of time can be hard. I do not recommend trying to take it on all at once.

Before you officially go back to work, try starting the separations for just a few minutes, then work up to a full workday. Go into another room, come back in, and tell your child what a great job she did for not falling apart. Then gradually increase the time between exits and entrances.

This will not *completely* eliminate the tears as you work up to the full day, but remember you are giving your child wonderful coping skills and this practice will serve you well.

Say goodbye quickly

With my daughters, saying goodbye at daycare was especially difficult on days when I left for extended business trips. I would build up the forthcoming trip, they would get anxious, I would feel guilty, and everyone would be unhappy.

As I knew travel would always be part of my job, I decided I needed to accept it and make a change that would make it more palatable for everyone. So, I turned to my daycare providers for advice. Knowing they had much more experience with separations than I did, I asked them how we could make saying goodbye easier.

Without hesitation, they explained that the most adjusted children have parents that make their departures happy and quick. They refrain from prolonging the transition and get their children quickly settled in a "no-nonsense" sort of way. Although I thought I was showing my love by sitting down, reading a story, or even watching Megan eat breakfast, I was actually only making our morning separations more difficult. I intuitively knew this, but because of my feelings of guilt, I hadn't put this step into practice.

Now, I help my children during morning drop-off periods by saying goodbye quickly and going on my way. This is the same whether I am going to be gone for just the day or for several nights.

"Separation" often begins long before the actual event (daycare drop-off) and its effect, if not managed well, can linger throughout the day. Saying goodbye becomes easier as your child learns to feel more secure, trusts you will always come back, and understands he or she has not done anything to *cause* your leaving.

Separations are not limited to daytime, so think about incorporating this principle into your bedtime routine as well. With our first two children, we tended to make bedtime a long production: lots of stories, last drinks of water, and adjusting nightlights until they were just right. With Parker, I think because we were more experienced and understood the benefits of saying goodbye quickly, we made the decision to set bedtime at 8 p.m.—without exception. If we had time for extra cuddles, then we spent that extra time together. But if it was late, we skipped those extra steps and Parker went right to bed.

Although it took me three children to get this right, today I have learned this valuable lesson and now, at daycare, I bring in Parker, get him settled, and get moving as quickly as possible. I strongly believe that learning to "say goodbye quickly" is the primary reason for our success.

Don't sneak away

I admit it. I used to do this. In the early years, I would enter daycare with Megan, get her distracted in her breakfast or some kind of activity, and when she wasn't looking, I would make my escape unnoticed.

Although I "won" in the moment by mitigating the drama from my exit, I lost over the long haul. I know now that what I was doing was teaching her that she couldn't trust me. Don't make this same mistake!

It is tempting, but while you may escape one morning, when she realizes that she cannot trust when you will stay or when you will go—it will only be more difficult the next time.

Instead, when she cries at your departure, just calmly say, "I know you don't want me to go, but I will be right back this afternoon. Let's wave goodbye together." It may take several mornings of following this routine, but she will come to depend on your exit and your return.

Let your child have some control

Everyone feels better when they have a say, don't you think? Although you need to leave and say goodbye quickly, consider letting your toddler "choose" some things that make the separation more tolerable.

When Megan was little, I would let her choose how many hugs to give me, or whether we said, "See ya later alligator," or just "Goodbye." By letting your little one take part in the planning, you reduce his or her anxiety, which will automatically reduce yours.

Another tip: give your toddler a small job. For example, try: "Hang your coat up for Mommy," or "Tell Mommy what seat you sit at during breakfast."

Don't be late

I am never late for a meeting with my boss, nor am I ever significantly late to a client visit, so why would I think it's okay to be late for the most important people in my life?

Sometimes the people we love the most are the ones we treat with the least respect.

Work can get crazy. The phone calls, the email, the meetings; the time can fly by and suddenly it is 5:00—time to pick up Parker. It is tempting to make "just one more" phone call, or answer "just one more" email. But if Parker expects me to pick him up at the end of a workday, and I don't show up until all the other parents have come and gone, it is much harder for him to deal with the morning goodbyes as I am setting him up for a long-term feeling that Mom doesn't always honor her promises.

If you struggle with being on time, consider setting your alarm fifteen minutes before you plan to leave for work as a reminder to begin wrapping things up and getting centered for the next day.

Don't come back until it is really time to come back

I have been there. You are standing outside that door and hear him crying. You want to go back in for "just one more hug." Don't do this. If you go back, you are telling your child that his tactics are working and you are rewarding him for less-than-stellar behavior.

Also remember: the day will come when you have an important meeting or phone call that keeps you from taking extra time in your departure. If you display inconsistency now, this will only confuse your little one and make his anxiety grow when you really need your routine. Resist the urge!

If it makes you feel better, go ahead and stand behind the door and surprise yourself at how quickly your child will calm down. Each child is a bit different. Of my three, Emily always cried the loudest, but also adjusted the quickest.

Don't buy gifts to cover your guilt

Two years ago, I was on a business trip that needed to be extended from three days to four. The timing was horrible—it meant that I would have to miss my daughter's parent-teacher conference for the second time that year.

In the hotel room that night, all alone, I felt frustrated with my job for keeping me away from my family, sad that I was letting down my daughter, and guilty for not being a "perfect" mom. When I finally arrived at the airport the next day, I was in a rush to get home to at least check in and hear how the conferences went, but no luck—my flight was delayed.

In my last-ditch attempt to make it up to my daughter, I started purchasing overpriced airport toys and candy. A few hours and fifty dollars later, I finally got home and gave Emily these "gifts." She liked them—of course, every child likes to receive presents—but it didn't make up for the fact that I had missed her conference.

It also reinforced the wrong message: that I had done something wrong when, in fact, I hadn't done anything wrong at all. This goes for goodbyes, too. Use words, not bribes, to encourage cooperation.

I've seen kids bribed with candy, toys, fast food meals, *anything* if they would just stop crying at the morning goodbye. It doesn't work. In fact, it increases anxiety by turning the goodbye routine into a daily test, and even worse- an expectation.

Life is full of obstacles and challenges. Be happy when things flow in your favor, but teach your children to know and expect that sometimes they won't.

Get into a routine

Another tip on accepting separation is acknowledging that the source of your child's emotions is often more centered on *transitioning* to something new and less about the actual separation itself. It isn't that they do not miss you (they do), it's just that your absence forces them to make a change.

Parker has problems transitioning in all kinds of situations, not just daycare drop-off. When he is watching his favorite television show and it is time to go somewhere, like a birthday party, he cries. When it is time to leave the birthday party, he cries. It isn't that he doesn't want to do the new activity; *it is just that he can't see beyond his present moment.*

Parker is a child that requires routine. He needs to get up at the same time, eat the same breakfast, and watch his favorite television show—all in the same order. He has only a handful of superhero shirts he will agree to wear. If I try to change any of these things, we always have some form of emotional outburst.

Because he thrives and depends on routine, I do my very best to keep it the same. So, on school days, we get up at the same time, have the same breakfast, and get dressed quickly. Then as a reward, we usually watch a few minutes of his favorite cartoon.

This difficulty in transitioning through change also applies to my older children. Every Monday morning, Emily seems to have a cough or a headache. I know that part of her aversion to beginning the Monday school routine is part acting, but more than anything it's her reluctance to move through the change from the weekend back to the weekday.

Now that I understand her challenge with change, I help her. I usually play along and tell her to get dressed and let's just "try school for the morning." We have an agreement that if she is still not feeling well after the first few school periods, then I will come and pick her up. Sure enough, once Emily gets to school I almost never hear from her.

Children crave structure even though they don't think they do. By establishing morning and evening routines you can help your children through many transitions: from home to school, from school to home, and from home to bedtime.

Check in at set times

When I travel to the West Coast, I wake up every day at 5:30 a.m. to speak with my kids before they get on the school bus. I feel tired from getting up so early, but these calls keep me connected and remind my children that I am always available even if I'm at a distance from home.

Travel is not part of all working mothers' timetables, but this tip applies to any type of work schedule—from a regular work day with a late meeting to an extended business trip. By checking in at set times you are effectively establishing a system both you and your child can depend upon and look forward to.

And, since guilt can grow when you have not connected with your children, this step will really make you feel like you are part of your family environment.

Prepare everyone

Part of easing separation guilt is to help get everyone prepared. It doesn't need to be difficult. I just do a few things to make sure my time away goes smoothly.

I make sure the fridge is stocked, there are clean clothes for everyone, and emergency contacts and calendars are updated. Please know, I am not suggesting you do every household task in advance of your departure. In fact, I have an entire chapter dedicated to partnership, and heading out of town is an example of a time where teamwork really takes effect. However, giving thought to these things and developing a plan will help you quell some of your feelings of guilt and make your time away from home easier for everyone.

Don't take it personally

All the time, I hear myself talking about how my girls are so different from one another. Emily is outgoing and theatrical; Megan is sporty and reserved. What makes one child fall apart and another wave happily when Mom leaves?

Personality and temperament are funny things. Just because your child cries at every morning drop-off and their friends get busy having fun doesn't mean that *you* are managing separations poorly. Kids are just different.

Ease *their* anxiety

Although it can be difficult, separation anxiety is a normal stage of development for children. Below are my favorite tips to help your little ones adjust and make the process easier.

Find a safe place

When Parker is feeling anxious, we pick a place he can go to just calm down, feel better, and get under control—in his own way. Good options can be as simple as a little corner in the classroom or just outside in the hallway. If you determine this space together, your child will feel like you are partners in this effort.

Help him look forward

Even when Parker was two years old and often hindered by vocabulary, he still understood much more than he could say. I did my best to prepare him for our departure by talking through (slowly) what was going to happen ahead of time. We would talk about where I was going (Mommy is going to work), where he was going (Parker is going to school), and when we would all be back home (at the end of the day).

We would also talk through all the details, such as who would be watching him and what his day was going to look like: you are going to have circle time, then a nap, then playtime outside, and then Mommy will come to get you.

Talk about the fun

Instead of focusing on your child's issues, remind him of all the fun he will have during the day and how much you are looking forward to hearing all about it when you return. "Parker, you are so lucky that today you get to play baseball, how fun!" Or, "I think today is movie day, make sure you really watch so you can tell me all about it tonight!"

Try a security object

They call them "lovies" for a reason. Parker has always had a favorite black teddy bear that we bring back and forth to daycare every day. Emily had a blanket, and Megan had a water bottle (don't ask). This security object can be a source of solace and comfort. If it helps, use it!

Always remain optimistic

Children pick up on everything. Even with my best game face on, Parker can tell when I am having a stressful day or when I am preoccupied with other things. Even tiny babies pick up on parents' emotions. Parent separation anxiety and guilt can often transfer to your children if you are not careful. Make sure you *never* make them feel guilty.

Give it your best to be optimistic, upbeat, and enthusiastic every single day. As a working mom, you may be more anxious than your toddler, so do your best to reassure him (and yourself) that you are making the right decision for your family.

Appreciating that separations are a part of life is a key step to building a guilt-free working motherhood. But it's also one of the hardest. For many mothers, it is something that will continue to be an ongoing process. Even today, it is still difficult for me to drop Parker at daycare, or say goodbye to Emily and Megan for a few days. But I keep trying, and the above tactics help.

And although I try to do everything right, sometimes I still make mistakes. Luckily, I know that part of my responsibility as a working mother is to teach my children that *it is all right if I am not always there*. Parker, Emily, and Megan have all learned to be comfortable without me, to understand that I will always return, and to see that their mother has a life outside of our family. Knowing these are important lessons has helped turn my separation anxiety into working mother confidence.

Four

Make
the Most of
Time
Apart

"Distance means so little when someone means so much."

Unknown

•Proud Working Moms Confess•

"If ever there is tomorrow when we're not together. There is something you must always remember. You are braver than you believe, stronger than you seem, and smarter than you think. But the most important thing is, even if we're apart ... I'll always be with you."

Sylvia

Sales executive and mother of two

"Sometimes things do not run as smoothly as hoped, but it is amazing to learn that my kids actually know how to load a dishwasher or clean their rooms—who knew? There may actually be a silver lining to this travel thing."

Heather

Insurance agent and mother of four

Four

•Make the Most of Time Apart•

Megan lost her first tooth, something we had been waiting to happen for weeks, while I was on a business trip. The daycare teachers were very excited and did the perfect thing: they sent me a picture. Yet, when I received the big news, I still felt a sharp pang of guilt that I wasn't there to witness it.

I felt bad, I felt guilty, and I once again questioned why I spent so much time working. But then I realized—this could have happened while I was at the grocery store or while I was filling the car up with gas. It didn't happen *just because I was working.*

Working or not working, you can't possibly witness every single milestone. Remind yourself of this before you let the guilt begin creeping in.

This chapter addresses what comes when the separation begins. Acknowledge that the goodbye is over … good for you! You have made it through what is likely to be the toughest moment of your time apart. Now let's look forward to the reunion!

Here are my best tips for making it from the moment after saying goodbye to the moment you are holding your little one again.

Use technology to your advantage

Technology has come so far, it is simply amazing. As you use technology more and more in the corporate environment, think about using those same tools on the home front and staying close with your little ones while you're away.

One of my favorite ways to stay connected with Parker is to bring his favorite Spiderman story in my suitcase when I travel. That way, I can read it to him over FaceTime before he goes to bed.

Of course, it isn't exactly the same as tucking him into bed, but it is a close second. We can laugh, we can look at pages together, and it helps us keep our bedtime routine, even if from a distance.

Skype is a great tool, too. I regularly use Skype to help Megan and Emily with their homework. Facebook is great for sharing photos (or keeping track of a teenager), and an abundance of smartphone apps make it easy to share and view pics or short videos while you're on the go.

There are a ton of tools available, and new ones are being released every day. I am certain that as I write this, I am already out of date. But the lesson is still the same: embrace technology and make it work for you.

Share activities while away

Recently there was a national study done by the Pew Research Center in which 1,500 school-age children were asked what they thought made a happy family. Surprisingly, they did not list any of the things you might expect young kids to say. In fact, there was little mention of material things like toys, fancy homes, cars, or even money. What was their number one answer? *Doing things together.*

For the last year, part of my routine with my son has been to sing songs together at bedtime. When I have to go away on a business trip, I keep this routine by singing to him over the phone while he lies in bed and falls asleep. I love that Parker still hears my voice, and hearing him respond makes me feel closer to home.

Likewise, Megan is an avid collector and has a great interest in rocks and archeology. While I am traveling, I make an effort to look for new and colorful examples of rocks from some of the places I visit. When I return, she is thrilled to have something new to add to her collection, and it feels great knowing that I am contributing to something important to her.

Let your kids help you pack

Again, if working motherhood requires that you travel, one of the best ways to feel connected when planning a trip is to ask your children to help you pack. If you are not traveling, but are still "separated" by your office job, consider letting your kids help you get ready for work.

Having your little ones help pack up your computer, stack your file folders, or even help prepare your lunch will go a long way towards making them feel included in your work life.

Another tip for helping them feel included is to choose a "special something" of theirs that you can bring with you and something they can hold of yours. When I see the friendship bracelet my daughter made for me, I feel much more connected, so I wear it when I travel.

Leave surprise notes

If an important meeting is keeping you from your daughter's school play or an out-of-town trip means you'll miss your son's soccer game, slip them a surprise note so that your child will know you're thinking of them.

I have been known to put an "I miss you already" note in the girls' morning cereal box, or a smiley face note under Parkers pillow. My daughters' school lunches are also great opportunities for something silly and fun.

My kids love finding these notes and I love hearing their excitement and happiness when those notes are discovered. This little step can actually make your absence viewed in a positive light: you are making memories while at the same time showing your kids that they're always on your mind.

Arrange a special outing with Dad

Eating out! Ice skating! Going to see a movie! Sometimes I think my kids *like* it when I go away because Scott will often try to do something a little special or different that is just for them.

Create something that happens *only* when you are away—like a living room sleepover or watching a movie with snacks after dinner. Moments like these can create lasting memories that your children will cherish for many years.

I know it is not always easy to do since often your spouse or partner is also working full-time. This tip is not intended to create additional stress or expectation—just an opportunity to make the time special.

Get engrossed in your work

Haven't we all heard the saying that you are most productive when you are most busy? You have made the decision to work, so now—get busy!

In the early years, my best days were the ones when I was slammed with work. I would feel productive and the hours would just fly by. When the day's end came, I was ready to take a break and was truly looking forward to seeing my kids.

Take these hours spent away from your children and put them to good use. Get productive, get promoted, and feel good about your contributions outside of mothering. Getting engrossed in work allows you to get away from focusing on your fears. This, in turn, helps reduce your guilt and anxiety, while also helping you feel more empowered and confident.

Do something you couldn't do at home

When I am not on the road, the last thing I want to do is take more time away from my family to sit in a nail or hair salon for several hours. (Unfortunately, I am learning that the amount of time dedicated to monthly upkeep is increasing as I get older.) And even though I don't want to waste time at home on these things, business trips allow me to pamper myself and expend some time on things I wouldn't normally do.

Some other ideas are watching entertaining TV, bringing along a good book, or ordering a chick flick that your husband didn't want to watch. Or indulge in some mindless entertainment, which I find helps make my time away much easier. (The reality show *Wife Swap* is my favorite.)

One of my better uses of time on the road was the creation of this book. Those evenings I spent in hotels were put to great use as I pursued something important to me outside of work—reaching other working mothers. (There was plenty of *Wife Swap* watching, too.)

Whether it's pulling out your laptop to write a book or simply watching mindless TV, think of something you wouldn't normally make time for at home and find a way to do it on the road.

Nothing can take the place of a mother being home at the end of every day. But with a little planning, creativity, and love, time away can be a manageable—or even a positive experience.

Once you feel better about your separations, your kids will feel better, too. For me, nothing beats coming home at the end of a workday or an extended trip to big hugs and kisses from my kids. It's a good reminder of why I work: to provide support for my family and a good life for the people who mean the most to me.

Five

Stop the Compare Game

"Be who you are and say what you feel, because those who mind don't matter, and those who matter don't mind."

Dr. Seuss

•Proud Working Moms Confess•

"I am embarrassed to admit that I get caught up in the trap of trying to keep up with the Joneses and trying to do everything. Sometimes I think my kids see the back of my head more than anything as we drive them to all the "right" places and buy them all of the "right" things."

Christine

Working mom of two

"I remember sitting in music class, watching a 10-month-old demonstrate physical milestones that my 19-month-old son was just getting around to. It was really hard for me."

Juliette

Owner of Cheerfit and mother of one

"Find a mother that you admire and ask if she'll help you, and then offer your knowledge to a mother who is struggling. Mine answered the phone and listened to me cry though 54 months of nursing my kids."

Becky

Sales representative and mother of three

Five

• Stop the Compare Game •

Your best friend is wildly successful. She is happily married, has four perfect children, an immaculate home, and makes twice your income. You can't help but wonder what she's done right, and what you've done wrong.

How many times have you measured yourself against someone else?

One of my most regrettable traits is that I used to compare myself to other women on a regular basis. In my personal journey to alleviate working mother guilt, I have realized just how negative an effect these comparisons can have.

My judgments have run the spectrum: I compared myself to other working mothers, stay-at-home mothers, and women who were thinner, prettier, younger, and had better clothes. I have spent endless time pondering my neighbors' decorating styles, my co-workers' incomes, and my high school friends' marital statuses. *Why?*

Maybe I wanted to feel better about myself—acknowledge that I had done some things right. Maybe I wanted to see that others had done some things wrong. And maybe I was just feeling guilty and wanted others to see me a different way.

As women, we tend to compare ourselves with others to get assurance that all of our time spent at home and work measures up to a mental report card we have created in our minds. Of course the problem with these internal comparisons is that they're based on small pieces of reality, not the whole scenario.

These comparisons are not healthy. Trying to erase working mother guilt while still comparing your life to the lives of others is like putting one foot on the gas and another on the brake. You're not going to get very far.

Instead, try these strategies to stop the compare game:

Tune out criticism

Recently I was on the phone with an old friend from high school that I hadn't spoken with in years. It was good to reconnect and catch up on our lives. After reminiscing about old boyfriends, the conversation shifted to our children.

She shocked me with an unsolicited comment (those are always the ones that surprise the most) about working motherhood. With a very casual tone she said, *"I never believed in putting my children into daycare. I could never do that to them."*

As you might expect, this caught me off-guard, not only because it goes against my own beliefs, but because she's my friend!

It was hurtful and shocking, but not something new. Sometimes even the people you rely on to be supportive may not agree or understand your choices. This was certainly one such moment where my friendship was being tested.

I had a decision to make. My first reaction was to defend myself, my choice to work, and my belief that using childcare was a good thing. From my defensive position, I thought my parenting decisions were better than the ones she'd made. I reasoned that even though I am away for more of the daytime hours, having a career allows me to give my children exceptional opportunities. I rationalized that my children have college funds, play on sports teams, and have seen parts of the world that my friend has not really been financially able to afford her children. I was frustrated and wanted her to change her opinion to mine: that I am a better mother *because* I work. But, trying to change someone's viewpoint never really works.

My second, and more reasonable, reaction was to try to view her perspective in a positive way. After all, it was honest. In actuality, she is right. I am not able to be there for every recital or every morning at the bus stop.

But just because I can't be physically present for every moment does not change the fact that I am still the main source of love and guidance for my children. I am a wonderful mother. In fact, there is no one better.

You may not agree with someone's thoughts or beliefs but if you can remove yourself from the emotion and try (really try) to understand where the thought is coming from, there may be a nugget of truth somewhere that you can learn from.

You should avoid nasty neighbors, co-workers, or judgmental stay-at-home moms who have a negative effect on your confidence. It sounds obvious, but actually putting this into practice can be difficult. At our core, mothers and women are all the same. We want people to like us, to agree with our beliefs, and to provide encouraging support. When this doesn't go your way and you face hurtful comments (and you will), simply *choose not to listen.*

Ignore the hurtful remarks from others, and rely on confidence in your choices. Appreciate well-intentioned relatives and friends for all the good things they bring to your family and leave the rest alone.

Surround yourself with other encouraging working mothers

The winter talent show that my nine-year-old daughter Emily was performing in was scheduled for the same day I had to be out of town for a client presentation. Needless to say, I was devastated.

Emily had prepared and auditioned with a hula-hoop routine to a Taylor Swift song. We were thrilled when she made it, and she pranced around the house, practicing and replaying that song so many times, I think *I* could have done the routine myself, if only I'd had the moves. The talent show was incredibly important to her and I was so proud of her for mustering up the courage to get on stage in front of her friends, parents, and teachers.

But my company had been working on a very important deal for months. It was finally getting ready to close. The date had been fluctuating but the key players had finally committed to the date—on the same night of Emily's performance.

I needed to be with my co-workers, and I needed to be with my daughter—at exactly the same time.

In the weeks leading up to the talent show, every time Emily practiced her routine, I felt sick at the thought of telling her that Mom wouldn't be in the audience. What kind of mother was I?

A planner at heart, I developed a strategy: Scott would record it and play it back for me on our computer later that night. The grandparents would attend, and my sister would be there, too. Although all of this support was helpful, somehow it still wasn't enough. I just could not get over the guilty feeling I had about not being there. I felt completely alone in my pain.

Then I remembered that *I am not alone.*

I phoned Jill, a friend of mine and devoted mother of two who also has an intense travel schedule. She suggested that I attend the dress rehearsal. *Why didn't I think of that?*

So I sat in the auditorium and watched the dress rehearsal performance. Emily was adorable and so pleased to see me there. And to my complete surprise, there were *three* other working women in the audience with me! As it turns out, lots of parents travel and while they also could not be there for the big night, the dress rehearsal was a pretty good substitute. But I never would have thought of it without Jill.

One of the very best ways to alleviate working mom guilt is to get to know other women just like you. No one but another working mom understands how hard it is to keep yourself together during a big meeting when your child has something special going on at school or is home sick with the flu.

Build yourself a support network of other working mom friends—it will be invaluable. These women can help you much more than you might think: brainstorming creative solutions to scheduling problems, listening to each other's struggles, and celebrating each other's successes. Foster these special relationships and you will find unique encouragement, support, and most importantly, friendship.

Don't turn parenting into a competition

Having a conversation with a friend the other day, I heard myself rattling off all the milestones Megan had recently achieved, such as making club volleyball and excelling in academics. I heard myself doing more of the same about

Emily: she's a great dancer, very smart, and a natural on the stage. It sounded braggy, even to me, and so I faltered on my words and immediately tried to take them back.

Maybe because I had suddenly remembered that my friend's daughter wasn't doing as well in academics, I realized (too late) how totally inappropriate my self-important comments were. I was unconsciously engaging in a competition of sorts, and an unimportant one at that.

Thankfully, being a good friend, she let me off the hook and assured me I wasn't making her feel less adequate by sharing my pride. This, however, led to a deeper conversation about the true root of why we boast about our kids' accomplishments even more than our own.

We came to the conclusions that all of our bragging comes from the importance we give to other people's views of what a "good" mother looks like. Somehow, if Megan and Emily succeeded—and excelled farther than their peers—I could rest easy knowing that I had done everything right.

With this realization came perspective and growth: even if both of my daughters were struggling or falling apart, I couldn't possibly love them more. I'd still be overwhelmed with pride! My need to compare came from self-doubt in my own parenting skills and the way other people perceived them. If you begin the compare game, your guilt will grow. Don't do it.

Remember that every child develops at different rates and in their own way. While Megan may be a great student, Emily may be a great dancer, and Parker might excel in sports (we're not sure yet). Either way, all of my children carry their own special gifts and talents.

Don't internalize your child's development. Know that, as mothers, although we support and encourage our children's growth, we cannot determine exactly how everything will turn out nor can we predict all the choices they will make right now or later in life. I am very proud of my children, but I am careful not to brag about them to the detriment of others.

The easiest way to eliminate these unreasonable comparisons is to stop them in their tracks. So, when someone brags about something exceptional and you feel they're really making a passive—but negative—judgment on your own parenting, shut down the conversation. Simply say, "That's great," or "Good for you." Remember, the issue really lies with *their* confidence.

Parenting is not a race. There are no winners and losers. Rather than compete to be the very best parent, focus on raising your children *your* way and on your own timetable.

Teach other women to be good working mothers

Unfortunately there are no courses on how to become a proud working mother. So we have to be each other's teachers.

Working mothers have taught me many invaluable lessons. Like how to juggle a meeting and a play date, strive to be the very first to sign up for volunteer opportunities (so you can pick the easiest ones), or hitting the dress rehearsal performance of a talent show if you have to miss the real thing.

You know much more than you think you do. Be a mentor and support other women in your position. They are struggling just like you once did.

As I reflect on why I have chosen to write this book and my most recent endeavor (a website for working mothers, ProudWorkingMom.com), I realize it is because I want to continue in my journey of supporting others who are just like me.

Offer help and support for others, then watch how your own guilt fades away!

Reflect on how far you've come

Instead of comparing or measuring yourself against other mothers in a negative way, reflect on who you are today compared to the woman you used to be.

How has motherhood changed you? How have your priorities changed? How has your career changed? Consider the incredible accomplishments you've had, both personally and professionally, since starting your journey as a working mother.

Give yourself credit for all of the great things you have done!

Constantly comparing yourself to others is a no-win situation. The effort is time-consuming and only results in depleting your confidence. If you look hard enough, you will always find someone who seems to do it better, quicker, or more effortlessly than you.

Instead, pay credit to your uniqueness and remember you cannot know or understand anyone else's situation, just as no one could possibly know yours. Be confident in your decision to work and keep your focus on having a happy life at work and at home.

Six

Outsource
Everything
You Can

"The best executive is the one who has sense enough to pick good men to do what he wants done and self-restraint enough to keep from meddling with them while they do it."

Theodore Roosevelt

"I've hired a non-profit meal service that also feeds the homeless (there goes any guilt!). I no longer have to do the cooking and my kids set the table. This arrangement works perfectly for our family."

Sandy
Attorney and mother of four

"I ask my babysitter to fold our laundry. She has the time and it really makes a difference in my stress level. The wash is one thing, but it is the folding and putting away that takes time."

Nancy
Creative director and mother of two

"For me, I was shocked to find someone who could and wanted to work for our family every day for just two hours a day. She helps me with all kinds of things: picking up last minute groceries, dry cleaning, and is a master at organizing projects. I learned not to pre-judge and assume that there was no one who would want to help."

Julie
Marketing director and mother of two

Six

• Stop the Compare Game •

One of my best memories about realizing the importance of getting help was at a birthday party for one of Parker's friends. The kids spent an hour playing on bouncy castles before settling in for cake and presents.

I stood among the other parents and struck up a conversation with a very nice mother. When I mentioned my schedule for the weeks ahead, she blurted out, *"I just don't know how you do it."*

How cliché. This comment is *so* common in working mom circles they even made a movie about it! It used to really bother me, but now I am happy to say that I don't dwell on this statement. I'll admit, from an outside view, my life looks really crazy!

I have three young children with various after-school commitments happening in different places often at the same time. I travel several nights a month for my job, which has its own set of responsibilities. And I have a super-hyper puppy that destroys everything from my kids' favorite toys to my most expensive heels.

In the past, when people have said, "I just don't know how you do it," I would respond with a smart or funny comment, and then change the subject.

But, the truth is, *I don't do it all.*

Instead of struggling to balance everything, I've learned to ask for help wherever I can. Instead of exhausting myself with the extra stress of household tasks, I utilize the services and support of people that are fully equipped to help me. I hire a handyman service to finish quick repairs at home and ask our nanny to pick up ingredients for dinner on her way to our house. I know it can sound very "diva-like." But it is actually just being resourceful.

Why is it so hard for mothers to turn duties over to others? Is it that we feel guilty or inadequate? Do we feel weak if we ask for help? Are we too proud? Are we afraid of relinquishing control? Are we scared of being judged? Or maybe we think asking for help is admitting defeat.

There are many underlying reasons why working mothers struggle with asking for help, but it's a necessary part of being a successful working mom. The unfortunate truth is that trying to do too much means that *the quality of everything we do is reduced.* Sooner or later, we just break down and realize that all that we're doing is not allowing enough time for what the effort is really all about—our family.

"I don't have anyone to help me!"

"Someone else just wouldn't do it right."

"It's easier to just do it myself."

"I can't afford to outsource anything."

We've all felt this way and said these things, but here's the reality: you are not new to outsourcing. Whether you realize it or not, you already delegate tasks on a regular basis. As a working mother, we effectively assign the care of our children to others when they go to school or spend time in childcare. We balance errands and chores with our spouse, sending whoever can most easily go to the grocery store, dry cleaner, or bank.

By further maximizing the support network I have, I make my life *a lot* easier. If the business world outsources to be more efficient, working mothers can—and should—do the same. Instead of feeling guilty for not being able to manage everything alone, find creative ways to delegate tasks; it will allow you to spend more quality time with your family. It's genius, really!

Over the years I have seen so many working women sabotage their careers by trying to do too much. We take on household duties, make trips to local stores, run errands, work a full time job *and* try to complete DIY projects because we think we can do and accomplish anything. But there's an important distinction:

We can do and accomplish anything, but *should* we?

Many working mothers tell me they simply can't afford to outsource or delegate. My response is that you can't afford *not to*. The more effectively you outsource, the more you can leverage your own time to grow your career and earn more money. The more you are able to leverage your career in the way you envision, the happier you will be, and the more time you will have with your family. Isn't that really what we're all aiming for?

Here are my five steps to outsourcing effectively:

Make a list of tasks you can delegate

To begin thinking about which household tasks you can delegate to others, ask yourself the following: *Which tasks do I find enjoyable and which are time-consuming and exhausting?* We are always more productive when we focus on the things we really want to do.

o Which household chores or errands are really necessary on a regular basis?

o   Are there people or services that can help you with any of your common responsibilities?

o   Which tasks do you really dread doing? Could you easily pass them off to someone else? Or reduce the time you spend on them?

o   Are there any household tasks that you truly enjoy?

o   How much time are you spending keeping current with household responsibilities?

o   Are there any ways to include your children in necessary tasks to make them more enjoyable?

o   What are some ways you can alleviate pressures and responsibilities that take you away from career-building, family time, or other activities you believe are truly important?

When I went through this exercise, my focus was on outsourcing any task that took me away from what was important to me: career-building or family time.

I found that the biggest time commitments outside of what I valued as important were domestic responsibilities—cleaning, cooking, and regular errands like dry cleaning, groceries, and driving kids to their weekly activities (and we have a lot).

Obviously, we all need to take on some domestic responsibilities to ensure that our household runs smoothly. But by honestly asking yourself how you can be more efficient and by utilizing the support networks and services around you—you will be able to run your home without running yourself into the ground.

Find a good fit

It goes without saying that all tasks cannot be done well by everyone.

My housecleaner would be terrible at doing our taxes and even worse at mowing our lawn. The trick is to play toward everyone's strengths before you assign any work to others.

For example, in the creation of this book, I made the mistake of using my website designer to help with the cover creation. I did this because I thought it would be easier—I already knew him, he had done good work for me, and although it was outside of his normal responsibilities, I thought he could do a good job. I was wrong—way wrong. We went through several versions, I spent funds unnecessarily, and together we ultimately realized it wasn't right. You would think that as the author of this book, I would have taken my own advice. But we're all a work in progress, right?

The cover was eventually completed, but I certainly wasted a good amount of time trying to fit someone into a role they were not skilled to do. By managing your expectations and theirs, everyone will be happier.

Breaking projects into smaller, manageable tasks makes it easier to find a good fit to do the job. It also helps you avoid dropping an overwhelming amount of work on someone new who hasn't yet had a chance to show you their worth.

Match tasks with strengths, and everyone will be happier and more successful in their roles.

Outsource your least enjoyable tasks

This seems obvious, but we don't all have the same preferences or strengths.

A friend of mine recently told me that she decided against hiring a housekeeper, one of the most commonly outsourced activities for working mothers. Her reasoning was that she actually enjoyed cleaning her home and found it relaxing. I thought she was crazy, but she explained that she liked the feeling of accomplishment she felt by personally taking her home from messy to orderly.

While I don't feel the same way as my friend, I can understand her point of view. Instead of looking for the easiest or most common things to delegate, identify the tasks that add stress to your life or could be done better, or more easily, by someone else.

Here are a few ideas:

Childcare drop-offs and pickups

Getting myself and three small kids ready for work and school on time each day is a major feat that is not easily accomplished in my house (or any other for that matter). For most dual-working families, this is the single most stressful time of the morning and evening.

Something that has worked well for us is asking a local teenager or family member to help with the childcare drop-off or pickup. If you can find someone who just wants to earn a bit of income (as you would pay by the job or by the hour), you can help another family by providing work and help yourself by reducing stress.

I'm able to zip out the door in the morning and leave my helper to get the kids off to the right start. For a few extra dollars a day, it is worth its weight in gold!

Kids' after school activities

For my family, the morning rush isn't the only chaotic time of the day. In any given week, we have a variety of soccer, t-ball, volleyball, cheerleading, and drama lessons. While all worthwhile, they all take time, gas, and coordination.

Make arrangements to attend the events that matter most and hire someone (possibly the same morning helper) to help you with the pre-evening driving needs. Also, try to make friends with other parents who may be able to share driving responsibilities. But be sure to return the favor!

Laundry and cleaning

My guess is if you walked outside and asked any woman on the street what they'll be doing on Saturday, more often than not, the answer would have something to do with cleaning.

It may seem extravagant to get hired help with this, but just think about the hours spent cleaning the house and doing laundry. That time could very well be better spent with your family doing much more meaningful and memorable things.

Cleaning up after the dog

As much as I love having Smasher, our two-year-old Golden doodle, his needs are not my first priority before and after work. I just don't have the time to walk him three times a day, let alone pick up after him in the yard!

Instead, I pass this task on to my kids as a part of their regular household contribution. But if your kids are too little, or just can't take on this task, consider having someone feed your dog, walk him, and take care of cleaning up the yard as well. There are many dog walking services that are happy to do this for just a few dollars a day.

Looking your best

For me, shopping is a *dreadful* experience. I don't have the time or the patience. Consider getting a personal shopper, giving her your sizes, likes and dislikes, and, of course, budget.

It sounds extravagant, but you can actually *save* money if you approach this task correctly. If you can find someone who takes advantage of sales, coupons, knows where all the good deals are, and manages returns and exchanges, you might be surprised at how reasonable and valuable this resource can be.

I have a neighbor who loves to shop. She even has a little side business catering to working mothers. Through this, she is able to find both cute and reasonable things for me, and it's massively helpful.

The little things

It is the little things that take up so much of a working mother's day. Consider some of the most time-consuming: travel arrangements, choosing other children's birthday presents, returning simple emails, handling UPS deliveries, or even scheduling appointments. *Personal assistants are no longer only for the wealthy.* It is amazing some of the tasks an assistant can help you with—without a heavy fee. Try using Elance for some of your online needs, and reach out to Craigslist for some of your local requirements. Make sure you think outside of the box and really let these people help you.

If you aren't able to afford an ongoing personal assistant, these services also will work as your personal "concierge" by transaction or project. Again, if these are tasks you dislike, the fee you pay to have them off your shoulders is well worth it.

Grocery shopping or picking up dinner

One of my least favorite chores is grocery shopping. I am not much of a cook and the idea of taking time away from the family to roam aisles for produce and chips is not something I want to do.

In most major cities, there are services that offer online ordering and home delivery. There are extra fees for this, but consider all the time you spend at the store—and the expense of those impulse items you *really* didn't need.

Consider heading to Costco or Sam's Club for ready-made meals. They aren't half-bad and work well in a pinch.

There are also a lot of services now that allow you to "create dinners" in bulk, freeze them, and then pull out as required (such as Dream Dinners and Create a Meal). This not only allows you to quickly create dinners that are tasty, but they can also be fun for the family to do together.

Get creative

There are plenty of ways to get help, but sometimes all you need to do is get creative about managing the time you spend on chores—or *don't* spend. Here are some examples:

Think allowance

Although I never expect my kids to whistle merrily while sweeping the kitchen floor, it turns out that they can do a lot of things to help out. In my home every morning, my kids make their beds, get their lunches prepared (except Parker, the four-year-old), and empty the dishwasher. And every night, they set the table too!

Giving your kids an appropriate allowance each week can be a beautiful thing. It helps to teach your kids responsibility and encourages your family members to contribute. It also teaches children the value of money—a crucial lesson for children and adults alike. So many children do not understand the concept of money management and when those same kids hit the early adult years, they're lost. Giving your child an allowance is a good way to teach them how to manage money from an early age.

Have a nightly clean-up time

After a long day at work, do you still find yourself cleaning up toys, hanging up coats, and emptying the dishwasher? Stop doing these things all by yourself! These are things even your three-year-old can help you do.

When I come home from work, I always start by politely asking for everyone to "do a sweep around the house." Together, we hang up our coats, put away our shoes, and pick up dirty clothes.

Trade services with other mothers

It's no surprise that time is a valuable commodity, so trade it with other busy moms you know whenever you can. This does not just mean sending your kids to friends' houses on play dates for a little extra time to yourself. Consider giving a nice bottle of wine to your stay-at-home neighbor if she can wait at your house for the refrigerator repairman or the plumber.

My very good friend will often watch my girls get on the bus in the morning if I have an early-morning meeting. In exchange, I will watch her children on a Friday or Saturday night so she can have an evening out with her husband. It works for me, and I feel good about my contribution, too.

Be clear and then let go

The key to being a good delegator is being clear. "Wipe the countertops" has several meanings to different people. To me, it means spraying the counters to clean off any food or fingerprints that may be present. But to my kids it means wiping off the counters with the edge of their sweatshirts, not thinking twice about what might be left behind.

Whether it's your kids, a babysitter, or a housecleaner at the outset of a task, be sure to explain the purpose of a job, as well as your desired outcome. Giving clear descriptions and explanations will put everyone on the same page.

Now, *quit hovering!*

When I first had Megan, someone told me never to criticize Scott for how he parented. "If he puts the baby in an outfit that you don't like, don't say a word. If he puts her stuffed animal in the wrong place or swaddles her 'wrong' at bedtime, let it go." Otherwise, he'd learn that I was the only person who could do things "right" and he'd never gain the confidence to take on these tasks. As it turns out, Scott has always been just as skilled—if not more—at many of these tasks. But it was still sound advice.

Once you have entrusted another person with a task and clearly explained the purpose and outcome, then you need to walk away. You have given someone else the authority and empowerment to complete a duty on your behalf, so let them do it. Don't be that mother that says, "You missed a corner."

Try to keep outsourcing on your mind as you go about your day. Think about what you are doing that could be done by someone else—a family member, a hired helper, or a service.

Anything that frees up your time and allows you to focus on more personally or financially productive tasks is a good investment! We have such precious little time, so do your best to make it count.

Seven

Build
a
Real
Partnership

"If we are together nothing is impossible. If we are divided all will fail."

Winston Churchill

"He does more than his half, I am very lucky. He gets up with the kids, makes breakfast, manages lots of the pickups and even reads bedtime stories"

Sheila

Marketing director and mother of two

"I love that my husband cooks dinner for us. It is so wonderful to come home and be able to just connect with my kids knowing that someone else is also able to help with getting the dinner on the table."

Nancy

Copywriter and mother of three

"We've been together for ten years and have had a truly wonderful equitable relationship where we work hard to balance our home and personal obligations plus our professional careers. This is a gross simplification of course—my point is, we consciously make an effort to be supportive of each other."

Heather

Medical assistant and mother of one

"We try to get away for at least two nights three or four times a year. Being alone makes you remember what you love about the person in the eye of the storm with you at home."

Jessie

Sales representative and mother of three

Seven

• Build a Real Partnership •

I usually travel for work every other week for a couple of days—probably more than the average working mom. And travel as a working mom is rather predictable, in the sense that at some point, either, before, during, or after my trip, I can always plan on someone asking:

"So who is watching your kids while you are away?"

The question comes from men. It comes from women. It comes from peers. It comes from fellow working mothers.

I am no longer surprised by the question; in fact, I expect it. When I answer, simply saying that the kids are at home with their dad, I often see that look in their eyes. It is disbelief, it is surprise, it is pity. It's all of the above. *Every. Single. Time.*

What is unfortunate about these reactions is that so many people still assume that just because I am the mother and I am traveling, I *must* be leaving my kids with my mother, or mother-in-law, or sister, or some other very capable female. Often not considered is the very real possibility that my husband is not only running the show, but in a very competent way!

The *real* success of my working mother life has always been about partnership. For our family, we have always "made working work" by depending upon one another and thinking about our work and parent commitments as equally important—*to each other.*

On the mornings I travel, for example, it is not uncommon for my departure to occur before anyone is even out of bed. This means Scott has to ready the kids, drop them at daycare and school, and still get to his job on time—and that's early!

Additionally, in the evenings when I am away, he has to manage multiple pickups, prepare dinner, take care of homework responsibilities, and prepare everyone for the next day. By anyone's standards, male or female, this is a ton of coordination.

Our partnership works because I reciprocate by taking on the majority of drop-offs, pickups, and various appointments on weekdays when I am working from home.

Very truthfully, if Scott and I had more of a traditional marriage, whereby the majority of household *and* parenting responsibilities fell upon only me, the professional role I now enjoy could never have materialized. Both my career options and the development of those options would have been severely limited.

Not to overdramatize the point, but because I have this true partner in life who has been helping along the way, my career has grown and blossomed. Because my career has grown, and I feel like I have a real partner, I am a much happier individual. It all works together.

How many of us have heard the phrase, "If Momma ain't happy, ain't nobody happy"?

Although the phrase is funny, it has some serious implications. The phrase implies that the majority of families still operate from a traditional perspective. Mom keeps the house organized and functioning. Mom runs all the errands. Mom handles the majority of the child rearing, and now … Mom works, too. *But where is Dad?*

The problem is not that moms and dads are both working; the issue is that in more cases than not, Mom is still doing the majority of the running around. Dad is there, but he is not really as involved as he could be. This is either because he chose to operate this way or because Mom reinforced this traditional standard and has set this expectation.

Still, when Mom is trying to do all the family stuff and work too … Momma ain't happy.

According to a recent analysis, the division of labor is still very uneven when a husband and wife are both employed full-time. Specifically, the mother still does 40% more childcare and about 30% more housework than the average father. In fact, the study said that only 9% of dual-earning marriages share housework equally.

This is extremely disappointing, but—if we look around—not surprising. Consider these facts:

o Working mothers are on the rise. In 2013, there were more working mothers, both full- and part-time, than ever before.
o Of households with children, 40% of those families have working mothers.
o Women make up 46.9% percent of the labor force as of 2012.
o 55.8% of all mothers with children under the age of one year are in the labor force.

Here's the good news: the role of what it means to be a mother, parent, and worker is evolving. The new modern American family is learning that we need to juggle work and family in order to survive. It is now becoming much more politically correct to have more-involved fathers and also less-overburdened mothers in parenting and household efforts. So as working mom numbers continue to increase it will only be a matter of time before all working people will be equally responsible for both income generation *and* household chores. This is wonderful news! Proud Working Moms, let's begin paving the way.

We must teach our companions what it means to be a real partner. Here's how to do it in ten easy steps:

List your responsibilities

A good first step is to keep a one-week log of everything you do around the house and for your family. Have your partner do the same. Then compare your lists.

o How do you each feel about the items on your list?

o Do you feel you operate from a partnership position?

o Are there things that jump out at you that could be more evenly shared?

o Is there any task you intensely dislike?

o Is there anything your partner is doing that you could take on?

This exercise can be eye-opening. Don't be surprised if your list is very long and your companion's is not. You are not alone in this, but you can change. By taking a look at what is really happening now, you are taking one step closer to a true partnership.

Divide and conquer

How many of us have watched television images of an inept dad who can't change a diaper, open a jar of baby food, or start a load of laundry? It is not the 1950's anymore. Expecting a real partner means you expect them to help out with all things evenly.

Unfortunately, major advertisers continue to launch campaigns imposing the stereotype of a stupid dad who is clueless in the home and a mother who seems to really enjoy cleaning while wearing heels. I don't, do you?

We know there are a ton of dads who fit this "dumber than a box of rocks" stereotype. Just don't let it be your partner.

Here are a few examples of things you could divide and conquer. Think about these and the many others tasks you could get your companion to help with:

Laundry: One parent does whites and the other does darks. Or, one parent does the washing and folding, the other puts away (my least favorite part).

Bill-paying: One manages the day-to-day stuff (credit cards, monthly bills), while the other keeps on top of long-term finances (college funds, retirement accounts).

Groceries: Keep a list on the refrigerator so that the parent who stops by the store can get everything at once. Or, if you've already mastered technology, use OneNote or Evernote, which are tools that allow you to keep notes on your phone. Make a page listed as "stuff to buy" and sync it with your partner. On the way home, whoever is closest is the one who hits the store.

House and vehicle upkeep: One parent keeps the house working (air conditioner, heater, major appliances) while the other is in charge of the cars.

Pet Stuff: One parent does the feeding, another does the scooping and walking.

Cleaning: One parent is the duster and sweeper, the other vacuums and tackles bathrooms.

Nighttime stuff: One parent takes control of dish duty, the other takes up the bedtime story, bath, and laying out tomorrow's outfits.

Cooking: Assign meal preparation to the parent who is home at dinnertime, and trade off preparation meals when you're both around.

Taking out the trash: On trash night (assuming you have weekly curbside pickup), the parent who is not putting the last child to bed gathers and hauls the trash outside.

General house tidy: In the evenings, whoever is not on nighttime duty can work on straightening the home for the next day.

Arranging health appointments for children: Make one parent the doctor coordinator and the other parent the dentist coordinator.

Delegate according to who has the time

Building a true partnership means assigning duties based on who is available, who has the time, and who is better suited to get them done—*not* who is the mommy or the daddy.

For example, the part-time worker could do the grocery shopping or start the laundry. Maybe the full-time worker can help out with some of the scheduling (it is amazing what can be accomplished on the phone during a commute), or pick up a few things on the way home.

On days when both Mom and Dad are available, communicate and decide who will tackle what. Remember, it should be based on availability, not who wears nail polish.

Assign according to who is more invested

I believe that dads can cook meals and change diapers just as well as moms can change a tire, a light bulb, or manage the daily finances. In truth, however, I will admit that I do not enjoy keeping track of our financial accounts, nor do I really want to focus on when the next oil change should happen on our family vehicle. But Scott does. Those are some of his strengths.

Conversely, I am much better at organizing the kids' rooms and going through their closets—pulling what is worn out, what doesn't fit, and organizing them by color. (Yes, I might go overboard sometimes, but I enjoy it!)

Some jobs may be more important to one parent but totally inessential to the other. In these cases, as long as there aren't a huge number of them, the parent who is invested the most should be the parent who does the task. However, the parent who is opting out of the task should recognize it is being done, appreciate the time and effort the task takes, and help out in other ways.

Don't ask for "help"

It makes my skin crawl when I hear a working mother say, "Dan is such a great dad, he really *helps out* with the kids."

Why wouldn't he help out with the kids ... aren't they *his kids too*? A real partnership reinforces that housework and child-rearing are both of your responsibilities. He is not helping out, he is doing his share.

Fostering a real partnership does not mean only that your partner must see you as having equal responsibilities, but that *you* must, as well. You have to expect a real partnership in order to have one.

We've established that you can't take on all the responsibilities of parenting—you need your partner's help. In the same way, your partner can't build a real partnership without *you*. If you aren't at this point now, work to change this mindset within yourself.

Don't be a martyr

Scott is amazing at taking initiative. Knowing that I feel more relaxed when my home is tidy and the toys are put away, I love it when I see him making the beds, emptying the dishwasher, stopping by the grocery store, or putting the laundry away (my least favorite household task).

In truth, he never puts our "show pillows" in the proper place, and often he will forget to buy one of my needed items for whatever diet I am trying out. But it doesn't matter. I love that he takes initiative without being asked or prompted.

I know that allowing him to do it his way is much better than forcing him to do it mine, *which ultimately would result in me doing it myself.* Don't be a martyr. Getting your companion to do his fair share around the house means you'll be less exhausted and less resentful.

Let him make some of the decisions

It is time to honestly ask yourself: are you comfortable letting Dad take on many of the decisions you previously tackled alone?

To begin dual-parenting, we must release our hold on some of the decisions we make every day. Think through your list of what I like to call "Mommy calls" and consider if you can transition them to "parenting calls."

As an example, can Dad make the decision for a sleepover without your input? How about scheduling birthday parties, or going shopping for back-to-school supplies or Halloween costumes? Think about what you normally take on, and ask yourself if you can allow your partner to help with these tasks more evenly. The benefits far out-weigh the trade as you get a real partner and the kids get an involved, hands-on Dad.

And remember to brag! Everyone loves compliments. If your partner is a real equal partner—tell him and everyone else who will listen. Boast to the women at the park. Praise your husband's parenting skills in front of his male friends. Be the example to the masses.

People are always asking me, "How do you get everything done?"

I proudly answer, "I don't do it alone. Scott and I are partners."

Don't undermine your own authority

"Just wait 'til your dad gets home!" I used to say.

"Ask your dad if you can stay up till midnight." Or, "He's going to be mad if you spoil your dinner with ice cream!"

I can think of more than a few times when Megan and Emily left their bedrooms a nightmare with clothes and toys spewing everywhere. I wanted to punish them, but the softy in me didn't want to be viewed as the bad guy. So, I let Scott deliver the bad news.

This wasn't fair and, more importantly, it undermined my role as mother and copartner. Don't promote an unequal partnership. Your actions and reactions are exactly as important as your spouse so don't undermine your own authority.

Present a united front

Last Saturday, after I turned down Parker's desperate plea at Target for yet another Nerf gun (I swear we have a greater variety than Toys R Us), he unsurprisingly approached his dad and asked if he could speak with him "privately" in the kitchen. Keep in mind that Parker is four years old. Alas, negotiating skills begin early!

Scott of course had no idea I had already denied Parker. So when he agreed to pick one up for him later that day for doing a good job cleaning his room, he unknowingly created a problem: good parent (Dad) versus bad parent (Mom).

This was certainly an impressive accomplishment by Parker, but also a good opportunity for us to show our unified front in parenting.

As you might expect, we circled back to Parker and let him know that when Mom says "no," there is no point in asking the same question to Dad. In fact, bad things happen when we do this. We returned the Nerf gun, which was very disappointing to Parker, but a victory for our parenting partnership.

Kids will be kids. Sometimes I think my little ones were put on this earth to test my limits, but I know I was made a parent in order to guide them in the right direction. If you and your companion cannot be a united front, your children will feel it, know it, and they will conquer you.

Never stop dating

It was 7:30 a.m. on March 19. Like every morning, my focus was 100% on getting the kids out the door and myself ready for work: suit, shoes, coffee, cereal, backpacks and the usual child negotiations, *"No, Parker, please don't bring my toothbrush to show-and-tell today."*

Scott was looking at me funny that morning. He finally gave me that expectant and irritated look, like I had missed something incredibly obvious, and demanded, "Well?"

I racked my brain. What was it? Was my skirt on backwards? Did I have doggy poop on my heel? Was I running late? I had no idea what was on his mind.

"Do you know what today is?" he asked with a frustrated tone.

"Valentine's Day?" I said hopefully. *No, it is March, Jennifer, keep thinking!*

"Is it parent teacher conferences?" I tried again. They do happen like every month, it seems. I know this isn't right, but I'm getting desperate. Try as I might, I can't come up with anything.

Scott rolled his eyes, and said, "No, Jen, it's our anniversary." Then he pulled out a pretty little package from behind his back.

I felt terrible. How could I have forgotten? We have been married for 19 years! Actually, it was easy. I have three kids, a full-time job, and lots of other "activities" taking over my brain: cheerleading, client presentations, t-ball practice, diverting embarrassing show-and-tell moments, and planning preteen birthday parties.

Like so many other working moms, I had let kids and work become our life. When Scott and I went out to dinner, we discussed the kids. When we were together on weekends, we were doing kid things. I'll even admit that there have been more than a few nights that one of the kids ends up in bed with us. It goes without saying that this does not inspire romance.

Scott is the greatest guy I know. Yet in spite of all of our together time, I realized that we hadn't really been spending much time together at all. I needed to make him a priority again.

As mothers, we often feel that our children need us more than our spouses do. As working mothers, we also sometimes put our jobs in front of our partners.

It's true that kids need to be fed, clothed, and cared for, but they do not need more of you than your spouse. Your job also needs your full attention, but not more than the most important people in your life.

Believe me, I get it.

But I also get how important it is that you make sure your marriage or partnership is not just about chores, calendars, and children, but also about fun. This is one of the very best gifts you could give to your kids. Your children will feel safe and loved, and you will be setting a strong example for their future relationships.

As working mothers, we often don't have clear role models of what a real partner is. The ideal partner cares about you, understands you, and helps you—with family, household, and even work issues.

As a working mother, if you don't have a real partnership, you will always struggle. You will stop growing—both in your career and your relationships. But, if you do live a real partnership, this companion will help you "work on you." And as we become more fulfilled in life, we are able to add to the happiness in others, too.

Eight

Get Working Mom Organized

"If evolution really works, how come mothers only have two hands?"

Milton Berle

"Ever since giving birth to my first daughter, now more than 15 years ago, I have blurred the lines between work and home. I have finally realized the key to 'making working work' is to become organized."

Sheila

Nurse and mother of two

"I got to the airport only to find out that I booked my trip to New York backwards. I think that says it all."

Jane

Advertising executive and mother of two

"This year, I have really spent time thinking about ways to get organized and all of this legwork has paid off. I now have more time for friends, date nights, adventures, and even relaxing."

Jennifer

Attorney and mother of two

"You need to have one calendar for work *and* home. Otherwise, there will be a day when you realize, all of a sudden, that in the next 30 minutes you need to be in two places at the same time."

Therese

Sales representative and mother of three

Eight

• Get Working Mom Organized •

I once had a co-worker named Lisa who was also a working mother of two. Lisa was always a mess. Her clothes were splashed with coffee stains, and her office had two desks piled with papers, knick-knacks, and data from the multiple projects she was working on. From what I could tell, none of her files were ever organized. Lisa was a great friend, but our work styles and habits were certainly nothing alike.

One morning, I had to come in early to find a file I needed for a presentation I was working on with Lisa. I must have searched her desk for more than half an hour, without any success. When Lisa came into the office later that morning, I asked her for the file. She reached into the middle of one of her stacks, and without taking her eyes off me, smiled, and softly uttered, "Duh, it's right here."

We all have our own organization systems. If you find that system and it works—my best advice on this chapter of organization is to stick with it. For those of you that haven't found a system yet or may be looking for some tips and tricks, I can help.

One thing is certain: working mothers feel rushed. No matter how organized we think we are, there will always be days when we can't find our car keys, a child suddenly gets sick out of the blue, someone can't find his favorite Spiderman t-shirt (even though you know you laid it out), and the dog *actually* ate your report.

While I definitely do not claim to be an organizational expert, I do strongly believe that it plays an important role in my happiness as a mother and a professional. When the chaos level is down, the calm can begin.

Unfortunately, as we working mothers know, in addition to our mommy to-do lists, we also have a long work to-do list, which means that we must make an effort to manage our time wisely. Staying organized is a key step in mitigating our guilt, as much of it stems from feeling out of control or being pulled in too many directions. When Mom is in control, the family is too.

The below are my top suggestions for home and work that have greatly helped me maintain organization—and my cool.

Wake up early

We are friends, right? Then let me be honest. I am *not* a morning person.

I don't relish the opportunity to pop out of bed when everyone is still in their cozy PJ's. I love to sleep, and have a special relationship with my soft pillows and my lush comforter. But as much as it breaks my heart to admit, an extra hour or even twenty minutes well-spent before everyone else is awake can make the difference between a great day and a frantic one.

Create cushions of time for yourself so you don't have to freak out, run around, or swear under your breath. Here are some great tips to make early mornings work for you:

Think portable

Eggs, pancakes, and oatmeal … none of these travel well for the working mom. Think of food that your kids can take along to daycare or eat in the car, at school, or at home—all *without the mess*. My favorite items that make the grade: bagels, frozen waffles, and Pop-Tarts. Look for drinks that fall into the portable category as well. Think juice boxes—you can even get similar small milk cartoons, too.

Make the best of "morning TV time"

I will readily admit to allowing ample TV time in the a.m., but I make sure to use it to my advantage. Parker is not the best at staying put. If I want to get things done, I will often turn on an episode of *Power Rangers* (thank goodness for Comcast's Xfinity On Demand) and get him dressed while he is still in his TV trance. The fights about outfits are often missed completely if he is dressed in full without realizing it.

Avoid morning chaos by getting ready the night before

As I have two full-force tweens, we help each other by laying out our "sparkling outfits" and packing school lunches the night before. This makes a *huge* difference in terms of reducing the morning disagreements about clothing and keeps us moving during our morning rush.

Another tween tip: have your kids shower the night before and brush their teeth in the shower—it works. Without some of these approaches, my girls would take two hours to get ready every morning.

In addition to getting up just a bit earlier, you can really reduce your stress level by spending a little time each night preparing for the next day. I write out a quick to-do list the night before, including all the things I know must be done in the morning. It really takes only a few minutes but brings so much more control to the day ahead.

Heck, you might even sleep better if you know that all is ready to go in the a.m.

Keep things where you need them

As your kids get older, the "important" things they need for their daily activities will change.

As infants, they always need baby wipes, formula, and diapers. But, as my children are getting older and heavily into sports, I seem to always require Band-Aids, ice packs, PowerBars, and a change of clothes. Regardless of the items they need, or their age, the principle remains the same: keep things where you need them.

For example, I have two plastic bins in my car. The first bin usually has some snacks—you can never have enough (no matter what age), baby wipes (another ageless product for quick clean-ups), and paper towels. In the second bin, I keep a set of clothes for each of my children. These bins are always in the trunk of my car and they have saved us more times than I can count.

In the same light, keep all your bath items in a basket near the tub. Parker always has his bath toys and swimming goggles (yes, it is true—he wears them in his bath every night). By having this bath bin, I am never tempted to leave him alone should I realize I am missing something.

Keep a family calendar

In our home, we call our calendar "command central." It lists everything—where everyone is going, at what time, and it extends for a full year. We keep it next to our phone and check it every night to be sure we know what is planned for the next day.

Our calendar has to be in pencil because we know we can't commit anything to pen, but I am not opposed to color highlights by family member.

In addition to my old-school approach of writing it down, there are also many great tools available online to help manage family time and resources. Refer to the "Resources" section at the end of this book for additional ideas.

Create a weekly schedule

In our home, we know that Saturday we pick up the dry cleaning and Sunday we pay the bills.

A great way to establish a clear routine is to have a written household schedule. To start, make a list of everything you need accomplished on a weekly basis. These items should include many of the obvious culprits: grocery shopping, bill paying, getting the mail, dog walking, and filling the cars with gas. Then, assign each activity to a day of the week.

Of course, all of these activities should *not* be done only by you (refer back to the chapter on "Build a Real Partnership"). By splitting time-consuming tasks and assigning them planned days of the week, you will be better able to keep your chores manageable.

Remember to also keep your older children involved in the schedule. Megan and Emily know they are responsible for keeping their rooms clean, making their beds, and emptying the dishwasher—every day. This alleviates the work my husband and I need to do at home, and also gives them a sense of ownership and responsibility.

Use a daily planning tool

I keep my daily planner with me at all times. It's small enough that it fits in my purse, and I keep everything in it. Anytime something comes up that I need to follow up with, *I write it down*. If it is not on paper, I have a horrible habit of forgetting it. Like most women, my mind is always running, and as a working mother, it's never focused on just one thing.

My planner is divided into sections: high and low priority. This is the place where I keep my short list of urgent tasks that I must get done and another list of tasks to accomplish later. It includes both personal *and* work items—I think of it as a roadmap to everything.

If you are more of a technology-minded person, consider using tools like OneNote or Evernote to keep track of your daily lists. Both are great systems that allow you to organize, prioritize, and synchronize with your phone, computer, or tablet.

Keep a clean workspace

I used to get so frustrated with how messy my desk was that once I actually swept my arm across the desktop and threw everything into the garbage. It might sound silly, but keeping my office clean saves me time every day, reduces my tendency to procrastinate, and helps me feel in control. A clear desk encourages a calmer state of mind and can go a long way towards boosting productivity.

Another workspace tip: buy fresh flowers every week. It is amazing how a simple burst of color and a fresh scent can keep you feeling upbeat and energized. My kids love to make fun of me for this, but it makes me happy!

Don't price-check or waste time with coupons

I love a good deal; we all do. But be careful that your good deal is really worth your time and effort.

Have you driven across town just to take advantage of a two-hour sale or a $10-off coupon? Consider how much time you spent driving to and from your money-saving venture, the gas you used on those drives, and the energy you expended fighting against the shopping crowds. When you add it all up, what did you really save? Anything?

Think about all the time you spend running around to different stores, trying to save 50 cents on milk, or five cents on a gallon of gasoline. It's not worth it. Assign value to your time and spend the extra few dollars, knowing that your time is best spent elsewhere.

Organize your home entryway

Have you ever wondered how your daycare or children's school can keep track of so many items for so many little people? There are lunches, coats, hats, mittens, and show-and-tell items (though hopefully no mothers' toothbrushes). *How do they do it?*

They have a system around their entryways (their busiest places), and they stick to their system without fail. So why don't we take a page from our schools and apply it to our homes (our busiest places)?

First, *create "coming-in" and "heading out" boxes.* In our home, we have a little bin set in our laundry room that serves as a place for incoming mail, keys, and quick purchases that have yet to be put away. Heading out of the house, we also have another basket that serves as a holding place for bills going into the mail, the dog leash, and returns to be made.

Second, *use cubbies and height-appropriate hooks.* At our house, each child has a separate spot for backpacks, boots, hats, and gloves. And instead of having Parker drop his coat on the floor every time he enters the house because he can't reach the closet, we installed a special hook at adult-waist-level, just for him.

Work while you travel

Since business travel is such a huge part of my work life, I wanted to address the topic of getting organized on the road. Without question, I get more work done and accomplish more critical thinking on airplanes than anywhere else. If you don't fall into this category, consider yourself lucky, and feel free to skip this section. But with 48% of people traveling by plane for business last year, it only makes sense that many of them are working mothers. Of course, the expectation of productivity is very high regardless of whether we're in the office or en route to an out-of-town meeting.

These are a few of my favorite tips for helping you stay productive while on the road:

Plan ahead

This means thinking about the tasks you'll complete and bringing all the materials you'll need. If you wait until you are on the plane, you won't be adequately prepared to do your work. I am constantly using my laptop during my flight, but during take-off and landing, use of electronics is not allowed. Instead of wasting that time, I bring along reading material or a group of tasks that don't require my computer or phone. Birthday party thank-you notes or holiday cards are great tasks that can be accomplished during those technology-free minutes.

Take advantage of in-flight Wi-Fi

Most major airlines now offer in-flight wireless connections for a small fee (usually about $5.00). This minor charge is well worth being able to stay connected. Over the course of a two-hour flight, I'm able to catch up on almost an entire day's email correspondence. By the time I land, I feel in control and accomplished.

Reserve a seat that lets you work

I always choose an aisle seat. I feel like I can stretch out a bit more, and can make it to the restroom without disturbing those around me. Everyone has a different seat preference, whether it be aisle or window, but either way, you will be more productive when you are comfortable.

Avoid the chitchat

If you are trying to get things done on your flight (although I reluctantly will admit you can make great business connections en route), the last thing you need is a stranger updating you on his mother's bunion surgery. I find that the best way to politely dismiss a conversation is to break out noise-canceling headphones or power up your computer as soon as you're allowed.

Control your email

Who hasn't experienced frustration trying to organize their inbox? On an average work day, I can receive more than two hundred emails (some I am interested in—many I am not). This isn't a shocking number, in fact, it may even be the norm. In many professions you can spend your entire day reading, filing, and organizing your inbox. But trying to manage and organize an inbox leaves very little time to actually answer questions or evaluate information being sent.

Below is my best advice towards keeping on top of your inbox:

Limit checking email to three times a day

This takes tremendous discipline to master. But once you decide to look at your inbox only three times during your work day—early a.m., mid-morning, and late afternoon—you will soon discover that most can wait for a response. By focusing your time on these specific periods, you will get more accomplished and while also training the people you interact with on how they can expect to work with you.

Turn off email notifications

Gasp! *What?* Unless your job demands replies within minutes, checking your email can harm your overall productivity. On average, it takes 64 seconds to fully recover from being interrupted by an email, according to a study done by Loughborough University. So, locate your "Settings" or "Tools" menu, turn off your "notifications" options, and save.

Unsubscribe from junk email

How much early morning productive time have I wasted deleting repeat newsletters and junk email? It only takes a few seconds to delete, but if I added this time up over the course of a year, it might be a few hours of time that could be better spent elsewhere. Look through emails that are currently in your inbox. For any that you don't read regularly, hit the unsubscribe link.

Schedule emails to be sent later

Working mothers: get productive! The best times to send emails are before work and during lunch hours. An email sent at 6 a.m. is *three times* more likely to get opened than one sent at 4 p.m. This is a great tip I use to coach my salespeople on prospecting for new clients. Making difficult business connections is easier before and after work hours when other roadblocks (like clients' administrative assistants and non-decision-makers) are not yet at work.

Be slow to jump into group emails

It's amazing how group emails will work themselves out when you don't weigh in on every issue. Instead of responding throughout the process, let people on group emails attempt to work out their issues first. Then, just read the last email in the chain; you will save yourself a ton of time.

Create email folders

Consider creating email folders to store client or project-type emails. Create folders called "Follow-Up," "Interesting," or "To-Do." This is where you will file the email from your inbox that piqued your interest and you would like to review in more detail—later. When you find the time, you can simply look in the appropriate folder and read the emails worth keeping. Make sure to delete those not worth your time.

Flag urgent emails

This way they will be easy to find in your inbox. Microsoft Outlook and Gmail both have several flagging and follow-up tools to keep you on track. I am a big fan.

Move completed email out of your inbox

It sounds so simple, but once you have read the email—either file it, delete, or move it into the appropriate folder. This way Inbox is only related to what needs your attention.

Stop filing emails—just answer or delete it

Stop spending time figuring out crazy filing systems. Use your built-in email folders or *delete* it! Remember: if it really is that critical and you accidentally erase it, you can always dig it out of the trash folder or ask for the email to be re-sent.

Write short

How many email novels have you received? I have a policy: if it is more than two paragraphs, I hit the delete button and call the offender. When writing emails, follow this same advice. Say what you mean, be clear, but use as few words as possible. Having said all of this, do not be terse and watch your tone, which can be problematic in business emails. I have been known to send an email meant to simply get to the point but that resulted in hurting feelings. There is a fine line in email tone; just make sure you are careful while being efficient.

Avoid social media sites

I know it is tempting to look at Facebook, Twitter, Pinterest, and Instagram, but you know those sites will suck you in and you will lose precious work time you cannot get back. Unless it is for a business purpose, avoid social media and internet surfing during work hours.

Choose one system

There have literally been entire books written about the subject of filing, this is *not* one of them. Beautiful filing systems are nice to look at, but the trick with any organizational system is to actually *use* the system you created.

I have seen so many working mothers try to carry a planner, use OneNote, and also send voice reminders. This is way too many organizational tools to keep track of! Choose one and stick with it.

What I have found works well for me is to create two filing areas: one for work things and one for household things. That's it. I try to stay away from folders within folders within folders and using naming systems I can't remember. My goal is to deal with papers now or throw them out, and then move on.

Master your phone

A recent study from the Pew Research Center for the Internet revealed that American adults use only a fraction of the features on their smart phones. Sure, smart phones make it easy to organize your contacts and make calls, but what else can your phone do?

Use the mapping features

The built-in maps feature on the iPhone as well as the Google maps app include a compass, the ability to pinpoint and bookmark any address you plan to return to, and, of course, a chart of your route to any destination. If you travel or drive to new places for work, consider a phone with a GPS feature that will guide you with turn-by-turn voice directions. You can also use the GPS feature to keep track of your loved ones—especially handy with teenagers. I always know where Megan is, and this gives me a great amount of comfort.

Learn to use voice to text or email

When driving or walking, I use the voice memo feature on my iPhone to craft and return a simple email without taking my eyes or hands off the road, or losing a step in my pace. I also often use this feature to send myself simple reminders like "pick up milk on the way home." The app on the iPhone is pretty basic, but there are plenty of other great apps available for download.

Use the camera

There is a saying that "the best camera is the one you have with you." These days, the camera on your smartphone is probably better quality than the point-and-shoot digital you keep in a drawer somewhere. It's even useful at the airport—when I want to remember where I parked my car, I take a quick photo of the floor number and location.

Get stuff done online

There are *so* many things working mothers can get accomplished on the Internet.

Consider doing all of your banking online—you can schedule automatic payments, check your account balances, pay bills, transfer funds, and even dispute transactions. My bank offers this service for free, as do many others.

Additionally, as a working mom, I buy as much as possible online. Children's birthday party presents, my kids' clothes, my clothes, office supplies, and even makeup. Avoid spending time walking through shopping malls with tired and hungry kids or fighting for parking spaces on the weekend. Instead, do your shopping from home in a fraction of the time. My personal favorite is Amazon Prime which is a great service that offers free standard and two-day shipping on eligible items.

Get your important papers in check

Consider spending a few hours getting your family's financial, legal, and medical records organized. Hopefully there are no impending issues, but when you're prepared, you will feel much more in-control and guilt-free. Here are a few key areas to be sure you have sorted out:

Retirement income sources

Gather all of these documents in one place so you know very clearly how much income will be available to you and your family through retirement. You are working for a reason. To prepare for today and to plan for tomorrow, make sure your papers are in check.

Life and death documents

We all hate to discuss these issues, but you should have clearly outlined how you would like your affairs handled both while living and after death. Have a fire-safe filing cabinet that houses all of these documents in one spot. This cabinet should include the following: Medical records, homeowner/tenancy paperwork, auto, life, disability and long-term care insurance policies, wills, birth certificates, marriage license, and Social Security cards.

Contact information

Gather all information for your family's needs. This list should include doctors, dentist, childcare numbers, immediate family members and neighbors, and people to call in case of emergency. You never know who you might need to call on for support and you want to make sure this vital information is as easy as possible to access.

There is no doubt that being a working mother can be a hectic business. That's why you'll find that some of the most disorganized people are working mothers. By that same token, some of the most organized people you meet will be working mothers, too. Because they already know the secret: get organized!

Getting working mom organized means you'll feel more on top of things in all aspects of your life. You'll feel in control of home while you're at work, and in control of work while you're at home. No matter how many papers, emails, activities, or bills your family produces, once you get working mom organized, everything will seem much less daunting—and then you'll be surprised how much more smoothly things seem to go.

Nine

Think
Progress,
Not
Perfection

"There is no way to be a perfect mother, and a million ways to be a good one."

Jill Churchill

"I hired a Batman for my son's birthday party and invited his whole class. He wanted a bat mobile too, just like in the movies. I actually thought about renting a black Porsche and a professional actor. Then, I remembered that he's five and a cake coupled with Batman party favors would be just fine."

Julie

Accountant and mother of one

"I have finally learned to lighten up, and I gain more by doing so. I now know it is not the end of the world if my kids are not in bed at exactly 8 p.m., or if they eat cereal for dinner. If this is the worst that happens, then I'm doing just fine."

Stephanie

Marketing executive and mother of two

Nine

•Think Progress, Not Perfection•

When I was a kid, I couldn't bear the thought of finishing in second place. I believed that I could do anything and never wanted to settle for anything less than the very best. This is probably why my career evolved into outside sales; competition feels comfortable to me.

The desire to be "number one" always motivated me to work hard at school and put forward my best at work, but it took me a long time to learn how to distinguish between *being* the best and *doing* my best.

My pursuit of perfection stretched far and wide. And it has gotten the better of me many times. I've stayed up too late on a school night making cookies from scratch for a bake sale. I've made handmade Christmas cards when I really did not have the time, the energy, or the skill. I even tried to sew a Halloween costume without ever having sewn more than a button! Why did I do these things? I was trying to be perfect.

Today, there is so much outside pressure to be a "perfect" mother in our society that it's almost impossible to avoid falling into the trap. We hold ourselves up to an ideal of homemade dinners, hand-sewn Halloween costumes, and over-booked family schedules.

This chapter is about letting go of your need for perfection in both the personal and professional areas of your life. By learning to be satisfied with store-bought costumes or limited commitments, you will have more time to spend with your family—and that's what really matters.

Contribute in your own way

I would love to be able to say that I attended every class trip, volunteered for all monthly events at my children's school, and raised money for several worthwhile causes— all while holding a full-time job. But the unfortunate reality is that I simply can't do everything. And truth be told, I don't really *want* to.

I enjoy working. I don't work because I have to; I work because I want to. And I understand that I'm very lucky to be able to say this, as many moms can't. So it makes sense, then, that if given the choice of working or visiting the local zoo with 30 nine-year-olds, I would choose work nearly *every* time. Do I love doing things like that with my family? Absolutely! Do I want to burn through my limited number of vacation days just because I see other mothers contributing this way? No.

A useful trick is to find tasks that utilize your talents and skills, but don't take a lot of time. Need someone to tally up something in a spreadsheet? Sure, in a flash. Have a school newsletter to be designed? I'm happy to put my desktop publishing skills to work! Want someone to raise some cash for a worthwhile cause? You are looking at the best girl for the job.

The advantages are two-fold when you choose tasks that utilize your skills: you can complete these volunteer jobs easily by playing to your strengths, and you'll still feel good about your contribution.

As working mothers we have so much to offer but so little time. Don't fall into the guilt traps of trying to do everything that some of your stay-at-home counterparts are more easily able to accomplish. Contribute in a way that works for *you*.

Stop over-scheduling

Something happened to me earlier this year when I looked at my daughter, Megan, who is in eighth grade. She excels in school, participates in many extra-curricular activities, and seems to have a very full social life. I am very proud of her. But one night, while I was helping her plan her weekly activities and finish homework, I noticed that she looked tired. In fact, she looked utterly exhausted. Seeing her in that moment made me realize we needed to cut back.

As my kids grow, we're constantly offered opportunities to do all types of activities. Swimming, cheerleading, karate, dance, volleyball—if we attempted to do all of them, I would constantly be in the car, writing checks, and in a terrible mood.

A lot of working parents feel the urge to "hyper-parent," to schedule healthy and educational activities for their children every minute of every day. I, too, have been guilty of this. But, through my own efforts of "progress, not perfection," I've taken strong actions to stop.

So, when it comes to choosing activities for your children to pursue, keep these general principles in mind to prevent a chaotic schedule:

Choose activities the kids want to do

I have spent so much time and energy trying to push Emily into swimming, my sport of choice when I was her age. But she just never enjoyed it, and getting her to practice three times a week was an incredible challenge. It was expensive, time-consuming, and frustrating for everyone involved.

Once I got past my own ego, I realized I should be supporting what my children *want* to do and not what I think they should be doing. Then they become more invested and have more fun. Sounds obvious, right?

Just take a simple and honest approach with your kids. Sit down together and pick out the activities that they *really* want to do.

Limit activities

A self-diagnosed overachiever, I always wanted my children to have the opportunity to try and excel at everything. But the thing is, in addition to all of the "doing," they need time to just be kids. Just like I need a night (or two) to sit and watch reality television, they also need a night to eat junk food and relax.

Try to limit your kids to one after-school activity held no more than three times a week. This may be a harder decision for you than for your kids. We tend to want our children to be involved in everything and learn every skill and hone every talent available. But they just can't do everything, and downtime is both precious and important.

Choose activities that are close to home

In my family, we have a rule that we will never drive more than ten miles for any weekly activity. Any farther than a few miles, and the activity changes from fun to complicated and burdensome. Your time is valuable, so don't spend it on the road.

It might seem all right at first, but once you've made that same hour-long trip multiple times (and, let's not forget, hit the same Burger King drive-thru multiple times), the real value of the activity may not be what you were hoping for.

Teach your kids to entertain themselves

When I was a child, my sister and I spent a lot of time at the playground across the street from our apartment. We hung out, built creations from rocks and grass, and got really dirty. There weren't agendas, lessons, or formal structures to our activities. Sometimes there were other kids there, too, but a lot of the time, we just entertained ourselves.

Today, our children are so accustomed to having structured time at school and extracurricular activities that they can become dependent on us for direction and entertainment. But if you let go of the idea that you need to keep your kids entertained all the time, you will give them a chance to get creative and discover the world on their own.

Once you commit, attend what matters most

Emily loves when I watch her cheerleading practices. She likes that I see her perform the choreography, and I think it's fun to watch. Megan, on the other hand, could care less if I attended a single one of her volleyball practices—and she has more than three a week. In fact, she would probably rather I'm not there to hover. For Megan, the games, not practices, are what are important to her. That's perfectly fine—it allows Megan to cultivate her skills privately and build independence.

Being there for your kids when it matters most to *them* will let them know just how much you care.

Limit adult activities

The rituals that build closeness—bedtime stories, walks after dinner, playing games, and simply talking with your children—can't happen when you are not around. As a mom with many personal interests of my own, I have to fight the urge to overload myself.

I already have work during the day, but I also want to exercise and participate in my own hobbies. On top of that, I like being busy with my family on weekends and also want a bit of downtime. But with only 24 hours in a day, managing all of this can prove difficult, if not impossible.

In this aspect of life, I apply the same general guideline I established for my children's activities: I limit my activities, and for me, that means only one night of kickboxing per week (not four).

Learn to say "no"

It feels like I'm asked to participate in everything, from sitting on parent advisory councils to organizing fundraising events. In the early years, my immediate response was always "yes"—until I realized just how exhausted I was. It is a rare working mother that has enough vacation time and personal days to actively attend every event happening in their local schools or communities.

Between parent-teacher conferences, athletic events, academic fairs, award ceremonies, and field trips, there is just not enough time. And with more than one child in a family, scheduling can really become a problem!

So why don't you just stop trying to do it all? Instead, contemplate some of the *advantages* of not being that "go-to" person every time:

Someone else will get a turn.

It's great to know that Scott and the grandparents can attend stuff, too. It helps take some pressure off of me, and it provides a chance for others to step in, be more present, and develop their own bond with my children.

Your child will learn to be independent.

Sometimes I find that when I'm in the room, my children act a bit differently. Parker gets a bit clingy, and Emily tends to keep checking in with me to be sure I approve of whatever she's doing. As crazy as this may sound, sometimes when we are absent, our kids can have better experiences! Through this independence, my children learn to form their own opinions and impressions.

You'll make other moms, and their kids, feel better.

I have a number of working mom friends. One of these is the mother of Parker's friend, Cade. Spending time with Cade has shown Parker that other mommies sometimes can't make every event either. As a working mom, it's easy to slip into thinking that you're the only one with obligations that conflict with school events. But people with different family structures and career choices struggle, too. Sometimes missing an event can actually make other mothers (working *and* stay-at-home) feel better about their own absences.

It's okay if you get it wrong

Several years ago while on maternity leave with Emily and while trying to keep a somewhat regular schedule, I made a mistake. I was sleep deprived, overworked, and running too fast, and I left Megan at daycare way past the 6 p.m. pickup time. I felt horrible.

As odd as it may seem, I know *many* working mothers (and fathers) who, on occasion, have forgotten to pick a child up. No doubt it feels terrible to everyone, but unless this is an ongoing problem for you, you need to cut yourself some slack and stop worrying about long-term emotional damage.

Sometimes, even though we are superheroes by day and night, we make mistakes. Don't beat yourself up about it. Let it go.

Simplify mealtime

During my maternity leaves, I fell into the habit of overextending myself and making everyone's favorite dinners every night. Cooking individual meals for each family member was my way of showing my love. In reality, I was just unnecessarily complicating my daily schedule while trying to be a "perfect" mother and wife.

Time for a reality check: we aren't perfect. No one is. Exhausting yourself trying to achieve an impossible level of perfection is no way to live or keep your family happy. Here are some ideas that can help you avoid traps like the one I found myself in:

Do not make different meals for different family members.
Instead of making three different dinners, make one and expect everyone to accept and enjoy what is provided. If your kids don't like the evening's dinner choice, they can always have a peanut butter and jelly sandwich. I grew up with one dinner choice, and I turned out just fine.

Invest in a slow cooker.

Crockpots are great for serving up wholesome meals with little effort. Toss in a few ingredients, turn it on, and leave it until dinner! The best part (other than having a warm meal practically make itself) is that your house will smell amazing! There are a lot of great one-pot or slow-cooker cookbooks available at the market, and buying one is a worthwhile investment for quick, easy, and delicious recipes.

Have breakfast for dinner.

My kids love this because they feel like we're breaking all the house rules. But in fact, I'm saving myself a ton of time! Eggs, pancakes, sausage—it tastes good at any time of day and it's quick and easy. Dinner doesn't have to be "dinner food." If it's healthy and the family is together, then that's all that matters.

There is always takeout!

When all goes wrong, or everyone is just too tired, don't feel a moment of guilt about ordering a take-out meal everyone likes. You can even make it fun and have a picnic on the carpet. We do this all the time, and a bonus is that the kids think we are super cool.

Sometimes it can wait

It was a Saturday afternoon and I had decided that I would organize the kids' closets. Our home was exploding with clothes that didn't fit anybody or were out of season.

I was getting all the bags and labels ready for what was going to be a productive (but pretty boring) day when Parker looked at me and said in his little four-year-old voice: "Mommy, can we go to the zoo today and see the monkeys?"

Are sparkling floors worth missing a lazy afternoon at the zoo? Is a well-organized closet worth giving up a movie night with your kids?

The challenges of being a good mother and partner can feel never-ending and overwhelming. By picking and choosing your battles, your life will be full of fun moments and memories—even if your closets do not pass an organizational review.

Don't take things so seriously

We all resort to "drastic measures" at some point in our parenting. I once lured my daughter to bed with a trail of marshmallows going up the stairs when she was a toddler. I also will admit to giving Parker handfuls of Skittles to fend off in-flight meltdowns during long trips.

Am I proud of these moments? No. These aren't things I do every day, but sometimes there are situations that call for out-of-the-ordinary action. I am not perfect; I'm just doing the best I can!

Don't be a victim

Recently, while on a business trip, I struck up a conversation with another working mother over dinner. She had been on the road for two days and she talked (endlessly) about how she had no idea how her family was going to manage.

How would Dad get the kids off to school? How would she get her work done? How would she get caught up on all the housework when she returned? As she was telling me her laundry list of everything she had to do, I realized that she was not really taking any action, she was just feeling sorry for herself. I walked away thinking that her self-pity was just making her situation worse. It froze her ability to be productive and left her feeling guilty for leaving her family at home.

You already know self-pity isn't good for you. You know that feeling sorry for yourself harms your friendships, your future, your health, and much more. As working mothers, when we let the pressure of life fall upon us and dwell on it, we become what I like to call "stuck in our situation." If we allow this, we can reach a point where we don't have the energy or motivation to move forward.

Our thoughts and actions create 100% of the results (or output) in our environment. Earl Nightingale is famous for stating that our lives are a *direct reflection* of the effort we have put forward: we get no more, nor any less of the contributions we make.

In order to be happy, we must never see ourselves as victims. We must take full responsibility for our decisions and create the very best life we possibly can.

Set your own boundaries

Alas, although I really admire and respect many of the leaders I have worked for, I can't think of any one of them who ever turned to me when a meeting was going long and said, "Oh, Jennifer, it's 5 o'clock; don't you need to pick up your kids?"

It's not going to happen. You need to set your own boundaries for start times, end times, vacations, and everything in between. This also goes for responding to email and phone calls. Remember, Proud Working Moms set their own paths.

Recognize when something is good enough

As a mother, wife, and employee, knowing when something is "good enough" does not mean settling for less or giving up my dreams. In fact, it's far from it. One of my dreams has always been to write a book and create a website that helps and unites women just like me. Has it taken me much longer than anticipated? Yes. Is it as perfect as I had envisioned? Maybe not. But I've given it my best effort—and that's good enough.

Mother Teresa once said, "It's not how much you do, but how much love you put into the doing that matters." Ticking items off your massive to-do list with great efficiency may feel fabulous, but stay focused on the big picture.

The key to happiness is self-acceptance. Appreciate who you are today, and strive for balance. Not perfection. Life is short and time is precious. To be a successful and proud working mom, you are expected to give your best at work, and do your best at home. That is all you can ask and expect from yourself!

Give yourself permission to let go of perfection. Have confidence in the fact that you are doing the best that you can right now as a mother, a woman, a wife, and a friend. Do the best you can, but don't let "perfect" be the enemy of "good."

Ten

Be
Present

"Do not dwell in the past, do not dream of the future, concentrate the mind on the present moment."

Buddha

"The best time I ever have with my four-year-old son is when I just sit on the floor with him and play. I am always amazed at his intelligence. There is no way I'd know that unless I spent time interacting with him where he feels most comfortable – playing on the floor of his room."

Heather

Teacher and mother of one

"As I begin each day, I remind myself to stay where my feet are. If I keep my attention on the place I am, I have a better chance of mastering the present. What's here and now is all there is, or so we're told."

Emily

Sales executive and mother of twins

Ten

· Be Present ·

Have you ever been speaking with someone and then noticed that they weren't actually paying attention? They were nodding along, but you could see that their mind was elsewhere. How often do you think about your work or your endless to-do list when your child is telling you about their day? Have you ever eaten a meal only to realize that you don't even remember what it was?

We've all seen people multitasking without paying enough attention to the things around them. And we've all been guilty of it ourselves. I know I have. Sometimes, it feels like it's the only way to manage our busy lives, but I promise there's a better way.

There is a well-known saying about parenting: The days are long, and the years are short. Being a working mother is tiring and sometimes frustrating. But regardless of your child's age, every moment is precious. Learning to balance work, family, and time takes practice and focus. Part of this balancing act is learning to be present and appreciating the moments that matter.

Yes, it's totally cliché. But it's also totally true. When you reflect back on these years later in life, what will you vividly remember? Will it be the meetings you attended or the spreadsheets you created? Will it be the errands that you checked off your list? I don't think so. The moments and conversations with the people we love the most will always hold the most meaningful places in our memories.

On this quest to explain to people how I manage to "do it all," I have learned that you can't do anything without being in the moment. If I could give just two words of advice, I would say: *be present.* Below are just a few more tips.

Be present for five minutes

Here is a challenge so simple that you might think it isn't even worth a try. But humor me, and let's see what happens. *Commit to being present with one person in your life every day this week for five whole minutes.*

I'm asking you to stay totally focused for the whole time. You cannot think of other things, multitask, think about your to-do list, or even plan what you will do or say next. Just simply listen. Look into their eyes and let them know that what they are saying is absolutely the most important thing in that moment.

Can you do this for five minutes? Well, it turns out it's not so easy for me. As a working mother, I have gotten really good at doing three or four or ten things at once. At first, I thought this was serving me well. But over time I realized that in actuality, I was not giving my full attention to anyone or anything.

Typing an email, talking on the phone, and half-listening to my daughter, while keeping my toddler occupied used to be my normal way of life. Honestly, all this multi-tasking was really quite exhausting and distracting as I was largely somewhere else most of the time. At work, I wasn't focused on the conversations at hand, and at home I was only half-listening to what was happening around me in a futile attempt to maintain perfection.

Make an effort to really stay present with the people in your life. I promise you will be amazed at how much you have been missing while you were "accomplishing."

Don't put too much focus on the future

We all think that focusing on "the next thing" will make us happy. "My life will be much better as soon as I lose 20 pounds," or "As soon as I get this project done, I will finally be able to take some quality time off with my kids."

There's nothing wrong with thinking about your future—in fact, having a purposeful vision of where you want to go and what you want to achieve is extremely important. But at the same time, focusing too much energy on what you want to happen, or what should have happened, results in missing out on what is occurring in the here and now.

Parker will only speak in his little four-year-old voice for a little longer. Emily will only want to wear sparkles in her hair for a few more years. And who knows how much longer Megan will openly share her boy-band crushes with me.

These conversations and moments are only here *right now*. We never know what the future holds, so we need to learn to appreciate the present.

Be grateful

A good friend I have always admired often tells the story of the man who cried because he had no shoes. That is, until he met the man who had no feet. No matter how big your problems may seem, remember that there is always someone else who is struggling more.

The beauty of gratitude is that it directly attacks self-pity. You simply cannot feel grateful and sorry for yourself at the same time; the two emotions are incompatible. By practicing gratitude, we begin to recognize and appreciate what we have.

One of the steps I take towards feeling gratitude in my decision to be a working mother is to keep a journal of all the reasons that working is a good decision for me. This may seem a bit simple, but having a physical reminder of the benefits of my choices is an easy way to focus on the positive when times feel tough.

Love your work ...

Ask yourself the following question: If you could do anything for eight hours of every day for the rest of your life and money were no object, would you do what you are doing now?

Let me ask the question another way: Are you excited by what you are doing every day?

If not, what are you going to do about it?

This is one of the most important questions we should be regularly asking ourselves. One of the biggest blessings of living in a democracy is the ability to pursue one's own path, and the amazing idea that all of us can achieve great things however we define them. But so often we get caught up in all the doing, we forget about the thinking.

Long weekends give me both the excuse and the reminder to reflect on what I am doing with my life as a working mother. Every year, I try to take a bit of time and assess what I have accomplished since this same time last year. Then I think about where I want to go.

Working and motherhood can often feel like we are living in a trade-off of sorts. Without question, survival and success are undeniably connected, and it can sometimes be frustrating and chaotic while at other moments deeply fulfilling and empowering. This is our life. This is what we live every day.

The important point to remember is that we all have the luxury of deciding how our day-to-day work life is going to be. Is it going to be fun and rewarding, or is it simply going to be a means to an end?

Work occupies a huge percentage of our waking hours and is often an equally large component of our self-identity. Life is too short to spend working if you do not enjoy it. In these times of reflection and because we are living in this wonderful democracy, we must remind ourselves that *we choose.*

When our work is out of alignment with our passions, our natural abilities, or our values, it's nearly impossible to be content. Take the time to find work you love. It's well worth the effort.

… But leave it at the office

It happens to me all the time. We have just eaten dinner and are settling into our evening routine when all of a sudden I remember that I forgot to respond to an email. Or I start wondering if I've gotten the response I've been waiting on from a client or salesperson. As much as I want (and need) a break from all the office madness that inundates my day, it can be tough to turn off my work-brain at night.

The most obvious step to breaking the shackles that tie you to work is to simply unchain yourself. In today's world, that often means disconnecting and connecting with the living.

I was recently at a business dinner with some clients. While we were waiting for our table, I started people-watching. I was surprised to see so many people paying more attention to their phones than their own dinner company. If you look around, you will regularly see people taking calls or responding to a text or checking Facebook—all while engaged in a conversation.

To limit the distractions in my own life, I turn off my work phone every night from dinnertime until the kids' bedtime. Even though it's only a few hours, time seems to pass more slowly when I disconnect. I'm not interrupted constantly and I can cherish the time I spend with my children.

Unless you are actually being paid to be on-call at all hours, you can, and should, disconnect from all company-issued devices every evening. If you absolutely must take some work home with you once in a while, try to wait until after the kids are in bed to tackle it. That way, even if you have to stay up later, you won't feel resentful that you missed out on precious time with your family because of professional obligations.

It certainly takes some practice to start, and the temptation to check your phone, Facebook account, or Twitter feed is tough, but the effort is worth the reward. The demands for attention may never cease, but you can control your response to these demands by making a concerted effort to keep technology from taking over.

Let your kids play hooky

Once a year, I let each of my daughters "skip" school so we can spend the day together. We go shopping, have a special lunch, watch a movie, and most importantly—laugh. These are memorable moments and I make sure that I am absolutely focused on our time together. We have no errands, no closets to clean, and I don't check my email. They *love* that they get to miss school, which makes it all the more unforgettable.

Take a day to reconnect with your kids' daily rhythms, talk about their friends, and really listen. Each of your children will always remember their special day with Mom.

Just listen and share
"Mom, stop interrupting me!"
Parker (before I learned to listen)

I used to think I knew my children so well that I'd finish their sentences. I was rushing, I thought I knew their perspective, and I thought I was being "efficient." I know now that even though they're small—and can't speak or decide as fast as adults—it still hurts their feelings and takes away their chance to be heard.

My kids spend a great portion of their day following directions. They're shuffled between tasks, and told to "pick up your clothes," "make your bed," or "be nice to your sister." I know that these constant commands can be very overwhelming. If I don't pay attention, I can easily get caught up in telling them how to finish a task or even completing their thoughts for them just so things will move along more quickly. Sometimes I move too fast. Sometimes I don't listen.

Instead of rushing through daily tasks, take the time to listen to your children, even though it takes a little longer for them to express their needs. At bedtime during busy weeknights, ask your children to share sad and happy moments from their day. You might be surprised by what they share in these few, undistracted minutes together.

Just like us, they have valuable things to say and they need to be able to express them. If you listen to your children as they share the small details of their lives, they will be more likely to tell you the big important things as they get older.

The same holds true for adults. As Steven Covey said so well in his book *The 7 Habits of Highly Effective People*, "Seek first to understand, then to be understood."

Taking the time to listen to your loved ones will build their trust in you, while also letting them know they are being heard.

Create family memories

One of my favorite memories with my daughter Megan is our annual Christmas cookie-baking day. We choose about five recipes, head to the grocery store, purchase all the ingredients, and then spend the whole day baking together.

When we're finished, we hand-deliver packages to our neighbors, friends, and relatives. Her sense of accomplishment is huge. And, more importantly, the time I have with her is precious.

Instead of going out, consider staying home and creating real memories. Rent a movie, have a sleepover in your family room, or camp out in the backyard. Create a family game night or choose a complicated recipe in a baking magazine and tackle it. Family memories don't have to be elaborate or expensive but they do need to be fun!

Here are some of my favorite family activities to get you started:

- o Do something silly—have a race around the kitchen or a water balloon fight
- o Plant something in your backyard or garden
- o Make hot chocolate and break out the big marshmallows
- o Build a fort with blankets

- o Go on a treasure hunt for something silly (like a toilet paper roll in a restaurant bathroom)
- o Create your own *Minute To Win It* contest and let everyone participate
- o Cook your favorite treat
- o Make a collage of all of your special vacations and hang it in your kitchen
- o Take the dog and your whole family on a walk

Give your kids a few minutes of you

I get it, at the end of the work day, you return home exhausted and your second shift is just beginning. We all have carpooling, events, practices, and errands. In all the busyness of day-to-day life, it's easy to leave special moments unnoticed. No matter how little time you may have, it is important to find even fleeting moments to make your children feel cared for and loved.

Being intentional with your time takes effort. I am lucky to be able to work from home when I am not traveling, so when my kids get off the bus at the end of the day, I always try and give them my full attention, even if it is for only 15 minutes. We get caught up, talk about their day, and have a snack—together.

It's a nice break for me, and my kids feel my interest. But don't forget to refocus—they get started on homework and I get back to work. This may sound like such a small amount of time, but many studies report a small but very focused attention is far more valuable than an hour of distracted time. Think about it: what do you remember about some of your most important conversations? I bet it was usually when you felt like you were really being listened to, when you felt important.

Below are a few of my favorite ways for working moms

to quickly and effectively connect with their kids:

- o Ask caring questions each day like "How was your day?" or "What happened in math?" or "Tell me about this picture you drew." This one is the most important—shut your phone down and really give them time to answer.
- o Wear the special something they made for you.
- o Proudly display their artwork in important places (my favorite is my home office).
- o Give lots of hugs.
- o Call home to give good-night kisses if you're out.
- o Take a walk together.
- o Let them stay up 15 minutes past their bedtime watching something special.
- o Read a book together.

Set aside special time for each child

Parker and I have a "special time" every night before he goes to bed. For 15 minutes, we read together.

If the phone rings, or we have a visitor, Parker knows I will say, "I am sorry, I can't talk right now, it is Parker's special time." When that does happen, he literally grins from ear to ear, knowing that he has my full attention.

For my girls, once a month on a Saturday night we have a special "date night." We get dressed up, go downtown, and have dinner—just the three of us.

Create special moments that belong just to you and your children.

Eat meals together

At least four times a week, we eat dinner as a family. Sometimes it's takeout, and sometimes it is pancakes and scrambled eggs, but the important point is we are together.

As my kids have gotten older it has become harder to coordinate our schedules, but dinner is our time to really connect. Our conversations around the table provide opportunities for all of us to bond, plan, and learn from one another.

One way I try to make family dinners extra fun is with mealtime activities. Let me share two of my favorite ones that are both silly and educational. If you don't care for the below, take a look online; there are a ton of great ones out there!

Pass the What?

This game encourages vocabulary-building. Serve the meal family-style, placing all of the food in serving dishes on the table. When anyone would like a helping of a food, they must ask for it. But here's the twist: you cannot use the name of the food!

Instead, you must give a description of what you'd like. So, instead of asking, "May I have some mashed potatoes?" you would need to say something like, "May I have some of the white, fluffy food that tastes good with gravy?" This has been a great way to get our family talking and laughing together at dinnertime.

Question Bowl

Before your meal, take Post-it notes and write questions on them. Consider your kids' interests and recent activities. For example, "Which country would you like to visit and why?" or "If you were on a deserted island and could only eat one food, what would it be?" The idea is to pick subjects that will start conversation at the table. For this activity, I let my older daughters help with the preparation and have them write a question or two to place in the bowl.

At mealtime, you take turns drawing questions from the bowl and reading them aloud. This is a lot of fun and promotes some great dinner-table discussions.

Pick them up from school and make it count

If you can manage it, pick your kids up from daycare or school once a month, or even more if you are able. Plan for it, put it in your calendar, and consider it as important as any work meeting.

As a child, my parents almost never picked me up from school as they were always working. But the few times they did were very memorable for me. So whenever I can, I try to be the one who picks my kids up. And then I do my best to make it memorable. We always do something fun, like a trip to the bookstore for something new, or even better—an ice cream cone!

Your children need you to be present and you need you to be present for your family's sake. Many years from now, you will all be grateful for the lack of distractions and the focus on the people you care about most.

Today's life challenges are entirely different than the ones your parents faced. Don't allow business and life to distract you from living your life in the present.

Eleven

Don't Forget About Yourself

"Being taken care of is nice. Taking care of yourself is even better."

Unknown

"It's hard to balance my time at work and my time with the kids. I don't have much left for myself. Doing dishes late at night so I don't wake up to a dirty kitchen is about the only 'me-time' I have lately."

Jenna

Executive and mother of one

"I take care of myself by getting up early enough to exercise before school and running on the weekends. I try to get plenty of 'me' time—like exercising, shopping, and going out to eat."

Cathy

Teacher and mother of two

"I get my nails done every three weeks. It is extravagant and it always takes a few hours, but I love the time where I am able to just read magazines, sip a coffee, and have someone ask me about my day."

Heather

Marketing assistant and mother of two

Eleven

•Don't Forget About Yourself•

As you should now be feeling confident in your decision to work, and you know your children are being well taken care of, we now need to turn to the necessity of taking care of ourselves. Finding an hour in your over-scheduled day can feel difficult and selfish. The idea of taking time for ourselves has become strange and elusive.

When you continually give your energy to others, there will be nothing left if you don't also put something back. So, as a working mother, you absolutely must learn to give yourself time to re-energize and refresh. In order to live my life to the fullest, I need to make myself a priority, and my guess is that you do, too.

I recently joined a program at a national massage company, my latest attempt to snatch some "me-time." My membership gives me a full hour, once a month, that I am committed to. Whether it's a facial or a massage, it is time I've set aside just for me. To be sure that I didn't lose this precious time to other tasks, I pre-paid the full year knowing I would lose both the opportunity and the financial investment if I didn't go. Guilt in reverse, I suppose!

Here are eleven ways for a Proud Working Mom to take care of herself:

Treat Yourself

We all know money does not grow on trees, but that doesn't mean you can't find ways to give yourself a little something special once in a while. Buy that pair of earrings you have been noticing, or splurge on the heels that you really don't need. Don't overspend, but get something that feels good for you.

My favorite splurge is a daily Starbucks. I have a perfectly great coffeemaker at home, but ordering that latte just the way I like it makes me happy. The $4.50 for my very complicated order is well worth it.

Exercise

I understand—there are many days where I am booked solid with so many meetings that I barely have time to use the restroom, let alone go out for a jog or a step class. But by taking the time to schedule exercise into my calendar, I am amazed at how much more I can accomplish in a day. It is true—I swear it.

After exercising, my head is clearer, I am in a better state of mind, and though it is hard to believe, I actually do have more energy. Creating time to work out can be challenging, so here are some ways I've had success making exercise fit into my schedule:

Make exercise a priority.

If I told you I'd give you an all-expenses-paid, month-long vacation to the place of your dreams on the condition that you exercised every day before departure, would you do it? Of course you would! You'd make it a priority!

If your schedule is already full, then something else will need to take a back seat. Because in the grand scheme of life, few things are as important as your health.

Consider putting exercise on your calendar, just like any other appointment, and treat it as such. Just as you would not miss a work meeting, don't miss these appointments you made with yourself.

Exercise first thing in the morning.

As already stated, I am not a morning person. But if I exercise right after I wake up, I feel more energized and prepared for the day. Additionally, getting exercise out of the way first thing keeps me from getting interrupted by kids, work, and all the rest of life's surprises.

My gym offers early-morning kickboxing classes. At 5:30 a.m. Total honesty: it's really difficult to get up and make these every day. But when I do, I feel energized and proud that I have accomplished something before my kids are even out of bed.

Life and work tend to get in the way as the day progresses, and knowing that I don't need to take additional family time away in the evening makes that early a.m. meeting with myself worth it.

Exercise while watching TV or reading.

The average adult spends 16 hours a week watching television. Shocking, but true. Get a good book rack for your stair climber or treadmill and catch up on your guilty pleasures. Just think: yoga positions, leg lifts, walking, and even stretching are all things you can do while reading or watching your favorite show.

Exercise while on the road.

Being away from home is not a good reason to skip your workout. In fact, it's the perfect time to get in a jog or a fitness class as the usual mommy and household demands are removed.

Exercising while out of town has another benefit: by making yourself a priority while you're away, you will be able to alleviate your guilt by spending more time with your family when you return. Do your best to avoid the long dinners and cocktails and instead use the time to focus on your health.

Combine playtime with exercise.

One of the biggest excuses I hear working moms use is that they can't exercise because they don't have the free time. It's hard to be "selfish" and go to the gym instead of spending time with your kids. Well guess what: you don't have to.

Instead, utilize your time at home and get everyone out for some exercise. I often pack up the kids and the dog and we go for a walk in the neighborhood. Or sometimes a bike ride after dinner. Do they complain when I suggest it? Yes. But once we're outside, I only hear their laughter. There is no TV show anywhere near as memorable as spending time with your family. And with everyone tired after spending time outside, bedtime goes a lot more smoothly.

Go to the doctor

A few months ago, I fell on my ankle. It was a pretty big fall, and I was certain it was a sprained, if not broken. If this had happened to my kids, I would have rushed to the emergency room, but for me? I just grunted, hit Walgreens, and bought an ankle brace for $15.

I figured it would be fine in a few days. I was wrong. After three weeks of "taking care of myself," which means simply going about my daily life (with the exception of running), my ankle was still hurting. I needed to go to the doctor.

So many working mothers I know are amazing at caring for every single family member, big or small, but when it comes to taking care of themselves, they let it slide. As working moms, our goal is to work and be moms for a long time. Take the extra precautionary steps needed to care for yourself and be with your family for the long haul.

When you set up an annual visit for your child, make an appointment for yourself too. Think about taking the whole day off and just making it about you: get to your dentist for a teeth cleaning and have your physical exam done. And then when it's all over, reward yourself with a mani-pedi!

Follow your dreams and learn something new

In addition to all of the day-to-day things we need to accomplish, staying connected to our dreams helps us become inspired.

One of my personal goals has always been to write something that would be a source of support and inspiration for other working mothers. I started brainstorming ideas for this book when I had only a few spare minutes a day. With a lot of time and perseverance, look at what I have accomplished!

You may not dream of writing a book, but whatever it is—whether it's learning a new language or playing an instrument—gaining a new skill can be very personally rewarding.

Spending time on your own, dedicated to learning something new, is a great way to improve your mood and boost your self-esteem. While you're benefitting yourself with personal development, you're also being a fantastic role model to your children. You'll teach them that they can learn to do anything they want, as long as they're committed.

Take a day off work

Oh, I hope my boss isn't reading this! If your guilt is really gnawing at you, take a day off work to spend with your children or on yourself. Whether we're catching up on needed rest, recharging our batteries with some time alone, or sneaking off to enjoy fun-filled activities, sometimes we've all got to blow off work.

It can be hard to ask for a day off. We feel weak, or perhaps ungrateful, or maybe we're just scared we'll lose our positions. As someone who has managed countless employees, there's one thing I know: happy employees are better employees and happy moms are better moms!

If you're run-down, over-worked, and running on empty, you're a detriment to your company, not an asset. Take a day for you.

Maintain your social life

Remember when your Friday nights were booked with cocktails and fancy dinners instead of baths, PG television shows, and bedtime stories? I never appreciated how much time I had to socialize before my kids were born! My husband and I still joke about it. What the heck were we doing pre-kids? We had so much time on our hands, and yet, we had no idea. After Megan was an infant, all I could do was take care of her and, if I was lucky, maintain some sense of order at work. When the weekend came around, going out with friends was out of the question.

As a mom with a demanding job and little time to socialize on weekends, it can be very difficult to maintain a social life. And yet, we all know that belly laughs with friends, honest advice, and genuine sympathy are saviors of our sanity.

We all know that connecting with friends is a key factor to our overall happiness. Gretchen Rubin, author of *The Happiness Project,* notes a study indicating that having five or more friends with whom to discuss an important matter leads a person to feel "very happy." Other studies have shown that strong social connections can actually help lengthen your life.

Here are some things I do to ensure that I can incorporate my friends into my already busy working mother life:

Arrange weekend dinners with other couples.

One of my favorite ways to stay connected with good friends is to have a couples' night. We have friends, as I am sure you do, with kids that are similar in age to my children. Our friends come over around 3 p.m., we have dinner around 5, and everyone heads home at 9 or so. The kids have a blast, the adults catch up, and all without the hassle of staying out too late and throwing off our routine for the rest of the weekend.

Coordinate weekday lunches with friends.

Optimize your work-time freedom and grab lunch with a friend. A few of my friends and I are so committed to this that we have a regular monthly lunch date. Unless there's an emergency, everyone needs to be there!

Bring your kids along.

This may seem contrary to the point, but if there is no other way to get you out of the house or office, then find ways to include friends and the kids, too. You might hit the zoo, go to the park, or get everyone out for a walk.

Get some sleep

I have always been a horrible sleeper. Calming teas, hot baths, sleep medication—nothing ever seemed to help. Like many working moms, when the house is finally quiet, it can often still be incredibly difficult to quiet yourself and get that much-needed rest.

I am certainly not a sleep expert, but it's common knowledge that most of us require between seven and nine hours of sleep every night. Here are some of my best suggestions for getting some rest:

Exercise.

We already talked about this, but my kids *never* have trouble sleeping, and I believe this is because we keep them active. Exercise keeps you healthy, keeps you thinking clearly, and helps with sleep. On the days I exercise, I sleep much better.

Stop working.

It is so tempting for me to catch up on work once the kids are in bed and the house is quiet, but when I start thinking about work issues, I'm certain I'll be tossing and turning all night. Turn away from your work; it will be there for you tomorrow.

Watch what you drink.

As a full-on caffeine addict, I struggle with this. If I could, I would drink coffee all day and night. The truth is that caffeine can actually take hours to fully affect your body. If you have trouble sleeping at night, think twice about your afternoon coffee break. The same goes for alcohol. Even though I love red wine, I have to be careful. While one glass helps me relax, more than that really does disturb my sleep later in the evening.

Make your to-do list.

About an hour before bedtime, make a list of the things that need to be done the next day. Write it down and then release it from your mind. Keep a notepad (or your phone) by your bed. If you do wake up and think of something, jot it down and then you can rest knowing that you can refer to it later.

Go to bed at the same time every night.

Ironically, one of the great advantages of being an adult is not having a "bedtime," yet I have learned that being consistent helps me stay on track. Do your best to not throw your schedule off too much on the weekends. Have fun, but keep your bedtime consistent.

Eat healthy

This is not a fitness book and I am certainly no expert on what to eat or what to avoid. I will not attempt to lecture on carbs, sugars, or protein. At the heart of it, you know what you need to do.

When we are busy putting in full days at work and at home, it's very tempting to order pizza, or microwave that meal just one more time. When you eat better, you feel better. Do the right thing and be mindful of what your intake looks like. You will be glad that you did.

Take breaks every hour

Sure, you can work a twelve-hour day, but you can't stay 100% focused all of the time. No matter how effective you are, you will get distracted and actually become less productive over time.

I have found that taking a five- or ten-minute break every hour helps me stay on task. Get up, step outside for a few moments, and get some fresh air. The change of scenery and moving around a little bit will help you regain your focus.

Take the weekends completely off

Working mothers rarely take their full weekend just to relax. Errands, housecleaning, kids and their activities—all these commitments seem to take priority. Additionally, if you try and catch up on work during your weekend, you'll get run down.

Every now and then it's good to take the weekend completely off from every type of work you do. This means no work email, no phone calls, no errands, and no cleaning. Just have fun.

Listen to music

Studies have shown that listening to music is one of the few activities that actually involves using your entire brain. All cultures listen to music, and there are many benefits— from memory improvement, to helping with stress management, to more focused attention, even to physical coordination development.

Personally, I have always noticed how music can change my mood. I know when I listen to upbeat tunes, I always feel a bit happier or motivated to get up and move. In the same way, classical music has a way of calming my frayed nerves. I like to have a playlist for each of my moods: angry, panicked, exhausted, and seeking motivation, depending upon what I need.

Like all moms, it's easy to fall into the trap of taking care of everyone but ourselves. Make sure you are being kind to yourself. It's a surefire way to ensure that you will be the best mom, the best worker, and a great caretaker of others.

Twelve

Be a
Proud
Working
Mom

"Life is to be lived. If you have to support yourself, you had bloody well better find some way that is going to be interesting. And don't do that by sitting around wondering about yourself."

Katherine Hepburn

•Proud Working Moms Confess•

"I am a better mother because I work."

Kristin

Sales executive and mother of two

"Like any working mother, I find it hard to have a social life. But ... my kids are so well adjusted. There isn't a brat bone in their body so I know I haven't done anything that bad."

Tina

Sales executive and mother of three

Twelve

• Be a Proud Working Mom •

I used to live my life without being true to myself. I used to concern myself with what everyone else believed was best for me. I let the opinions of family, friends, and even neighbors shake my confidence as a working woman and as an adult. Looking back, I think even portrayals of happy families in the media may have influenced the way I lived.

We all know many happy, well-adjusted people that have been raised by working mothers. It is a myth that children who have a working mother are deprived or have a lesser experience than children with mothers that stayed at home. However, if we agree with this belief, or feel guilty and fearful, then chances are our children will also grow up with this mindset. You see, it's our *perceptions* of life's events, not the events themselves, that have the greatest impact.

I choose to work. I am a competitive person and a perfectionist, and I no longer apologize for this. I'm also crazy in love with my children and I will do whatever is necessary to be the very best mom I can be for them. Just like you, I still have moments of temptation … if I gave up my career, I could have a lot more time. My hair would be perfect, my nails would be done, and my body would be in much better shape.

But I would not be myself. I would not be taking advantage of the college education I worked so hard to earn. I would not be an equal participant in the relationship that is so important to me. I would not be as accomplished in a world that often focuses on the tactical and material. I would not be giving my skills and talents to a group of people, to an enterprise that is bigger than me. And lastly ... I would not be able to look Parker in the eye and say, "Kids go to school and grown-ups go to work."

For me, this is not being true to myself. So here is your final step in your journey to a guilt-free working motherhood: be a Proud Working Mom.

Eliminating guilt begins—and ends—with changing our belief that we somehow need to "make it up" to our children. We don't need to apologize for working, we just need to give our very best every day.

By reframing our mindset to focus on the benefits of working motherhood, we will shed our guilt once and for all. The last step in this process to becoming a proud working mom is to remind ourselves of the many reasons we work.

Here are my favorite reasons to be *proud*!

Being a great role model

My career shows my children something they can aspire to be in their future. As their mother, I am acutely aware that I am one of their primary role models. While my girls may not choose a path similar to mine, they will have grown up seeing that they have many options available to them. The choices I've made about living my life will guide them as they make choices about their adult lives.

As for my son, he will grow up learning that running a family is not "women's work," but that it takes everyone working together. Parker will grow up to respect women as equals in both the workplace and at home. And he will be a supportive and understanding man when it comes to his partner's career. For this, I am very proud.

Contribution to finances

My parents were not planners and there was never enough money for many of the things I am happy to know my children take for granted today. We had no college fund, they had no real savings, and there was no clear plan for retirement. This is not an unusual story.

For many years, my husband and I have jointly made great efforts to build college saving plans for our children and retirement funds for ourselves. I hope that one day these extra steps will help my children ease into adulthood without any financial burdens. And eventually, when Scott and I retire into our old age, I hope we can do so without putting any financial strain on our children.

Bringing home a paycheck makes me a contributor to my household, and makes me feel like I'm on equal footing. Like it or not, money makes the world go round. By working, I am actively reducing my family's risk of financial instability in the future.

No permission needed

Almost every morning, I stop at Starbucks and get a latte (sometimes a glazed doughnut too). It's a daily splurge, but working every day affords me a little luxury.

Once a year, I take my girls on a weekend somewhere fun—just for us. We stay in a hotel, we go to a few nice restaurants, and we go shopping. The fact that I bring income into our home gives me the freedom to make personal purchases that I might not feel right about if I were not contributing too.

Amazing experiences

Last summer, my girls went to a series of overnight volleyball camps. They played, honed their skills, and made some real memories. And every March, we plan a family vacation and go somewhere really cool.

As I look back at pictures of my children skiing, fishing, or ice skating, I am grateful that working makes me able to give my family some of these experiences and opportunities.

Independent children

As a working mom, there are times when we will be apart from our kids. It's that simple. Sometimes it is just for hours, other times much longer. Either way, my children know that I will always come back.

Since I'm not constantly hovering over them, my children are learning to become independent and confident. And, in turn, this makes me really proud of them—and myself.

Regular adult conversation

One of my favorite conversation topics always has been, and always will be, my children. Megan is a little pre-teen and constantly raises a new set of issues to keep me sharp. Emily loves to be at the center of attention. Parker is adorable and entertaining and completely caught up in a fantasy world of superheroes.

While I love talking with other moms about their children, it is nice to have a built-in break from this chatter. Sometimes I *want* to talk about customers, reports, current events, and even a nice dose of office gossip. Working keeps me balanced.

Much-needed time alone

One of my "happy times" is when I get to enjoy a peaceful cup of coffee while working each morning. By contrast, I can remember days on maternity leave when I was unable to even go to the bathroom alone. Working affords us time to think in quiet and focus on something other than the nonstop requests and needs of my children.

(I get to) wear nice clothes

At home I can't seem to keep anything clean—on myself or anyone else. If Parker needs to wipe his hands after finishing a snack of Cheetos, then what better place than directly on my shirt?

While getting dressed for business is sometimes exhausting (I don't enjoy putting on pantyhose any more than everyone else), it is nice to make it through the day without being covered in dirt and crumbs. While I might spill a cup of coffee once in a while, I can definitely say that I have never had a co-worker spit up on me.

No perfect home here

Working full-time and then coming home to a busy house full of children does not leave a lot of time for keeping an immaculate home. These days, I get a little help, but if I don't feel like dusting, or deeply cleaning the house before visitors, I can just tell everyone: "I really apologize for the way my house looks, I have just been so busy at work!"

Now, I do love having a clean house, it makes me feel more organized and in control. But it's nice to have a built-in excuse. My work obligations have excused me from housework more than a few times.

Pats on the back and "Atta girl!"

Raising my children gives me great pride, but work can provide a more tangible sense of accomplishment. When prompted, Parker will say thank you for laying out his morning cereal or his batman costume, but he is not able to give me a thoughtful annual review, a promotion, and certainly not a raise.

I love how I can accomplish and complete complex projects at work, meet goals, and really see the outcome of my initiatives. I am also quite fortunate to work with a great staff, including leaders that appreciate and acknowledge a job well done.

A stronger marriage

As night approaches and Scott and I settle into bed, we spend time catching up and talking about our day. These moments are absolutely precious.

Our dialogue often brings energy to our married life because we both have passionate connections to our careers and life outside our home. When we brainstorm about problems at work, discuss exciting projects coming up, or share our accomplishments at the office, it lets Scott and I continue discovering each other in a new light. We're able to connect and bond about things besides the kids and it keeps our marriage full of respect and pride for each other.

An identity beyond "Mommy"

I have said it many times throughout this book: being a mother is my most important role. But that doesn't mean I don't also want to have a deeper sense of self.

I want to be known in a context separate from my life at home with my family. Whether a stay-at-home or working mom, each one of us is multi-faceted, and being a mother is not the only way you should define yourself or be your sole purpose for being. Working allows me to identify myself as something different, separate, and independent from my family.

No one said it would be easy. But I know that the greatest gift I can give my children is a positive outlook. Being true to myself—ambitious, energetic, and driven, both at home and in my career—teaches my children that if they work hard, they can live their dreams as well.

After much discussion with friends, family, co-workers, and other working mothers, I have learned one very important thing. At the end of the day, all of us are just doing the very best we can. There is no right or wrong way to balance your career and your family. But life isn't really about finding the right way to do everything; it's about doing what's right for you.

Be a Proud Working Mom. I know I am.

Acknowledgements

I'd like to express my gratitude to all the wonderful people who have helped me get my work done in the midst of chaos, deadlines, and mom responsibilities.

I would like to give a big thank you to my sister (and working mother) Juliette Sawyer. Without you continually cheering me on through the creation of this book, it may have never come into existence.

Also, deep thanks to my friend and business partner Julia Romanow. As working mothers and friends, together we have done great work refining the direction of this book as well as realizing the need for ProudWorkingMom.com, a site dedicated to the empowerment of working mothers across the globe.

To Scott, my husband and partner in crime, thank you for putting up with me every day. That is no small feat!

To Parker, my lovely son, may you one day follow in the footsteps of your dad and be every bit as helpful—a true partner.

Lastly, to my daughters Megan and Emily, the true reasons I wrote this book. Without you to inspire me every day to share this message and set an example, I never would have been able to craft something so meaningful. Girls, the sky is the limit for both of you. Don't ever forget it!

• About the Author •

Jennifer Barbin has spent 20 years in the workforce, 13 of them as a busy working mother. She is Executive Vice President of Sales for a multi-million-dollar printing company, but can also be found at school events, practices, games, and driving groups of preteens from one activity to the next.

Realizing the issues working mothers face were universal, she founded ProudWorkingMom.com, where she shares experiences, tips, and suggestions to help working mothers gain confidence at work and at home. *Guilt be Gone!* is her first book.

Jennifer resides in Castle Rock, Colorado, with her husband and their three beautiful children.

Proud
Working Mom
Resources

For more help on any of the topics in this book, visit us at ProudWorkingMom.com!

And if you struggled with any of the steps in this book, here are some other valuable resources that will further guide you on your journey to perfecting working motherhood.

On childcare:

BabyCenter: A great place for advice with several articles on finding great childcare.

The New Parents Guide: More great articles on the all-important childcare decision.

On outsourcing:

Merrymaids.com – A great site for finding home cleaning professionals in your area.

HomeAdvisor.com – Online listings for trustworthy home improvement professionals.

AskSunday.com – A virtual assistant for outsourcing tedious tasks.

GetFriday.com – Another site for hiring virtual assistants.

Elance – Great site to find skilled freelancers in a variety of areas.

HireMyMom.com – A place to find freelancers who also happen to be working moms just like you!

On building your partnership:

Try *I'd Trade My Husband for a Housekeeper: Loving Your Marriage After the Baby Carriage* by Trisha Ahsworth and Amy Nobile.

For advice on splitting the workload: *Getting to 50/50: How Working Couples Can Have It All by Sharing It All* by Sharon Meers and Joanna Stober.

For organization:

Cozi – An app designed for managing a busy family.

Evernote – Helps keep everything organized and in one place.

OneNote – Kind of like a notebook on the go!

For online shopping:

NetGrocer.com – Order groceries and have them delivered right to your door.

Safeway.com – Another great site to have groceries delivered.

Amazon.com – There's *nothing* you cannot find here.

Diapers.com – They deliver diapers to your doorstep!

On your work life:

The 4-Hour Workweek: Escape 9-5, Live Anywhere, and Join the New Rich by Timothy Ferriss.

Successful Women Think Differently: 9 Habits to Make You Happier, Healthier, and More Resilient by Valorie Burton.

Project Eve – A great site all about women in business and female entrepreneurs.

On being present:

The Mother Huddle – A multitude of ideas for activities with the kids.

Today'sParent.com – Useful tips on making your children feel loved.

In general:

Parenting.com

WorkingMother.com

WorkingMomsAgainstGuilt.com

ProudWorkingMom.com

And if you liked our Proud Working Mom confessions, you might enjoy *Dirty Little Secrets from Otherwise Perfect Moms* by Trisha Ashworth and Amy Nibile!

Connect with Proud Working Moms on Twitter at @PWMBlog and www.Facebook.com/ProudWorkingMom!

Made in the USA
Middletown, DE
04 February 2015